MOST WANTED
PROFILES OF TERROR

MOST WANTED: PROFILES OF TERROR

OTHER LOTUS TITLES

MOST WANTED

PROFILES OF TERROR

Introduction by **K.P.S. Gill**

General Editor
Harinder Baweja

Authors
Rahimullah Yusufzai
Harinder Baweja
Amir Mir
Subir Bhaumik
R. Rajagopalan
Zafar Meraj

LOTUS COLLECTION
ROLI BOOKS

Lotus Collection

© 2002: Authors for their respective pieces
K.P.S. Gill • Rahimullah Yusufzai • Harinder Baweja • Amir Mir
Subir Bhaumik • R. Rajagopalan • Zafar Meraj

This edition first published April 2002
Second impression October 2002

The Lotus Collection
An imprint of
Roli Books Pvt Ltd
M-75, G.K. II Market
New Delhi 110 048
Phones: 6442271, 6462782, 6460886
Fax: 6467185
E-mail: roli@vsnl.com; Website: rolibooks.com
Also at
Varanasi, Agra, Jaipur and the Netherlands

ISBN: 81-7436-207-X

Typeset in Photina by Roli Books Pvt Ltd and
printed at Pauls Press, Okhla, New Delhi-110 020

Contents

About the Authors

Rahimullah Yusufzai

Rahimullah Yusufzai is a 48-year-old Pakistani journalist based in Peshawar, capital of the North West Frontier Province bordering Afghanistan. He has covered Afghanistan since the early eighties and was the first journalist to report the emergence of the Taliban Islamic Movement and interview its reclusive leader Mullah Mohammad Omar. He interviewed Osama bin Laden in December 1998 and had met him in the Khost camp that was later attacked by US cruise missiles. Mr Yusufzai was also the only journalist allowed to visit this camp before and after the US attack. The author also works for the BBC, ABC News and *Time*. He won the award for the best English columnist in Pakistan in 1985. He is presently the executive editor of the English daily, *The News International*. He is the joint author of the book, *The Past, Present and Future of Afghanistan*.

Harinder Baweja

Till recently an Associate Editor with *India Today*, Harinder Baweja earned a reputation as a committed reporter for her prolonged coverage of the insurgencies in Punjab and Kashmir. A close watcher of events in Pakistan and Afghanistan, Baweja also wrote *A Soldier's Diary*, a well-acclaimed and definitive account of the Kargil war. She won the Prabha Dutt award for investigative reporting in 1995 and in 2000 won a fellowship at Washington DC's Henry Stimson Centre where she wrote a paper on Kashmir and Third Party Mediation. She is presently working as Managing Editor, Current Affairs, Roli Books.

Amir Mir

Belonging to a family of journalists, Amir Mir is the founder of *Weekly Independent*, a recent enterprise launched from Lahore that promises 'a radical publication of opinion with reverence for facts'. He began his career in the nineties with *The Frontier Post* and in subsequent years worked with nearly every leading newspaper in Pakistan. He also had stints with UAE's *Gulf News* and Saudi Arabia's *Arab News*. Apart from getting his publication out every week, he has been working as *Outlook's* Lahore corrrespondent since 1995.

Subir Bhaumik

The BBC's Eastern India Correspondent, Subir Bhaumik is the author of *Insurgent Crossfire: Northeast India*. He is a Queen Elizabeth Fellow of Oxford University and an acclaimed expert on North-east India, Bangladesh, Bhutan and Myanmar. In 20 years of journalism, Bhaumik has trekked to remote rebel bases in the region and developed acquaintances with many top rebel leaders, including Paresh Barua.

R. Rajagopalan

He started his career with *Dinamani*, a Tamil daily of *The Indian Express* group, in the late seventies. He met LTTE leader Prabhakaran three times in Chennai and Delhi. He has first-hand knowledge of guerrilla territory in Jaffna and reported on the World Tamil Conference Against IPKF Oppression held twice in London. He specialises in Tamil Nadu affairs concerning the LTTE and the Cauvery water dispute. He broke the story regarding the Indian government banning the Indian cricket team from going to Colombo in 1986. The author's most important scoop was the Justice Milap Chand Jain Commission report on the Rajiv Gandhi assassination in 1996. He presently works as the Chief of Bureau of *Vaartha*, the second-largest circulating Telugu newspaper.

Zafar Meraj

A law graduate from Aligarh Muslim University, Zafar Meraj started his career as a reporter in 1975 for the Urdu daily, *Aaina*, edited by the well-known Kashmiri journalist and parliamentarian, the late Shamim Ahmad Shamim. In 1980, he switched over to English journalism when he became a reporter for Press Trust of India. Later, he headed the Srinagar bureau of *Kashmir Times*, a Jammu-based English daily for over eight years. He also contributed to *The Guardian* and *Financial Times* (London), *India Today*, *India Abroad* and *Independent* (Mumbai). The author has been contributing to *Outlook* since its inception in 1995 and has worked for *Zee News* and *Aaj ki Baat*. Presently, Zafar Meraj edits *The Kashmir Monitor*, a widely circulated English daily published from Srinagar.

Editor's Note

Terrorism is often referred to as India's threat number one. Indeed, the country has seen serious assaults on its democratic institutions, including on the Red Fort and Parliament House; both symbols of independent, democratic India. Two of her most protected Prime Ministers – Indira Gandhi and Rajiv Gandhi – have been assassinated. Punjab chief minister Beant Singh was blown to pieces while others like Farooq Abdullah in Jammu and Kashmir and Prafulla Kumar Mahanta in far away Assam have had narrow escapes.

Terrorism has spread its tentacles far and wide, be it through the groups operating in Kashmir in north India or the ULFA in the North-east or even the LTTE whose lethal capabilities have ensured that J. Jayalalitha retains tight security irrespective of whether she is in power or not. Planes have been hijacked and blown up, foreigners kidnapped and killed and vital installations bombed. The lethal Chinese assault rifle has often given way to improvised explosive devices that have been used to blow up bridges and army convoys; just as suicide bombers have now raised the threat of terrorism to alarming proportions. The Indian government has its own list of twenty 'Most Wanted' terrorists whose extradition they are seeking from Pakistan. This book profiles six militants who through their respective organisations hold out the maximum threat to India's unity and integrity. Interestingly, five of the six – with the exception of Paresh Barua, commander in chief of ULFA – are operating from outside the country's geographical boundaries. Some, like Professor Hafiz Saeed, the Lashkar-e-Toiba chief have never even set foot on Indian soil but yet control and command one of the most lethal terrorist outfits. Well-known counter terrorism expert KPS Gill's introduction gives an insightful overview while the other authors have profiled leaders of six important militant organisations to provide rich, often frightening details of their modus operandi. The six are 'most wanted' not only because of their past activities but also because of the threat they continue to hold out.

Introduction
K.P.S. Gill

In the rising discourse on terrorism, two parallel distortions are recurrently manifest. The first of these is visible in many 'academic' analyses of a range of terrorist movements, and is based on a process of substantial, if not complete, abstraction from the real world, from the identities and character of the principal actors, and from the unique motives that impel individuals to adopt the path of extreme violence. Such a concept is rooted in a largely mechanistic conception of the dynamics of social conflict, where a peculiar pattern of root causes or structural imperatives give rise to socially transforming violence. Writing, in a different context, on revolutionary violence, one commentator thus proposes that 'any valid explanation of revolution depends upon the analyst's rising above the viewpoints of the participants.' This is well in keeping with the general Marxist perspective that traces the roots of social violence and the revolutionary impetus to impersonal and entirely inanimate social and economic forces. The political agents who articulate and execute such violence, within this perspective, are purely incidental, generated out of the historical imperatives and social contradictions of a particular age and its disjunction with existing or emerging means of production. These arguments, developed over a vast literature on revolution have, over the past decades, been seamlessly transferred to terrorist movements, even where these have little in common – in terms of causation, or the origin, purpose and character of violence – with the classical or Marxist notion of revolution.

The second distortion, more apparent in the writings of journalists rather than of university scholars, or in images projected through various mass media – including popular films and television – swings to the other extreme. Here, individual terrorists or leaders of terrorist organisations are often glamourised, creating and projecting iconic images, immensely larger than life; or reflecting rigid stereotypes based on shallow preconceptions and personal sympathies. Calculated political violence is often transformed into the acts of unhinged psychopathic killers.

Archetypal images of unconstrained evil, remnants in our collective consciousness of the cautionary tales of religious mythology, express themselves in exaggerated profiles of individual and shadowy terrorists. Alternately, populist and shallow psycho-babble, the justifications of a neglected childhood, of early trauma, of poor socialisation, of parental abuse or oppression, emerge as favoured 'explanations' of inexplicable acts of intemperate violence against the innocent.

Both perspectives lie at a substantial distance from the reality of terrorism. The academic refuses to engage with the harsh and complex realities of the field; the popular writer is often blinded by his proximity to the action and to individual players in these conflicts, even as he attempts to grapple with an overload of incidents and events, as well as an unrelenting succession of deadlines.

In a long experience with terrorism, the weaknesses of both these approaches have been more than apparent to me. The 'root causes' thesis is as barren in its predictive capabilities as is the quest for the dominant terrorist personality. I have had the opportunity to interact, negotiate, confer with and question terrorists at different levels of their organisations – from ideologues and commanders to the footsoldiers of these movements – and have found as enormous a variety in their personalities, their subjective motivations, their personal histories, their comprehension of ideology and their idea of their own roles as was possible, and this great diversity made virtually all generalisations meaningless. There is, however, one generalisation that is borne out by empirical evidence – the motives of terrorists are seldom quite as elevated as many academics, as well as human rights activists and other apologists for terrorism, would have us believe them to be. This was more than apparent to those who were directly engaged in fighting terrorism. The venality of the terrorists was, for instance, uncovered in the wake of Operation Black Thunder, when evidence of routine torture, rape and a continuous succession of murders committed in the hallowed precincts of the Golden Temple in Amritsar was uncovered. This was borne out further by a confidential socio-economic profile of terrorists that the Intelligence Wing of the Punjab Police carried out in 1991. This study, which included 205 hard core terrorists, indicated that a majority of those who joined voluntarily did so for the lure of easy money and the 'benefits' attached to being a terrorist; more than a third of the non-hard core terrorists, moreover, were recruited by coercion. A previous criminal background was seen to provide a distinct advantage in climbing the terrorist hierarchy. Families of hard core terrorists, such as Gurbachan Singh Manochahal, Dharam Singh Kastiwal, Paramjit Singh Panjwar, Resham Singh Thande, Mahesh Inder Singh, Nishan Singh Makhu, Yadwinder Singh Yadu, Baghel Singh Dehriwal, among others, were identified as having amassed great fortunes. Even the lesser terrorists gained immensely in social significance and status once they had a Kalashnikov in their hands. Heads of their families were respectfully addressed as *Baba* in their villages and were approached for assistance in settling private disputes. Fathers of some of the better known terrorists set up independent businesses of extortion, mediation in cases of kidnapping, and a variety of other acts of intimidation and coercion. They also became beneficiaries of forcible acquisition of lands and other properties. Even if their sons died, they acquired the halo of martyrs; their families were called *shaheedi parivars*, and continued to receive substantial financial support.

These findings subsequently received independent corroboration that established that the primary motivation for terrorism was crude profit, or the supplementary fruits of the illegal power that militancy conferred. Three academics of the Guru Nanak Dev University in Amritsar, Harish K. Puri, Paramjit Singh Judge and Jagrup Singh Sekhon, on the basis of a survey, determined that that the 'fighters of Khalistan', after 1987, were largely social dropouts whose motive for joining the movement was described as *shaukia* – for fun. They observed that hardly three per cent of cases surveyed were 'found to have taken to violence out of anger against some kind of injustice . . . virtually none appeared to have had a political or religious orientation or was concerned with issues of injustices with the Sikhs and the problems facing the agriculturist farmers which were normally associated with the "Punjab Crisis".' The main causes identified for the terrorists joining the Khalistan movement had nothing to do with religion or ideology: 'At least 180 of the 300 terrorists we sampled joined "out of fun." The phrase that was often used was "*shaukia taur se*". They were happy if they had a motorcycle, a Hero Honda, (the 350 cc Enfield Bullet had been banned) and an AK-47, and if they got to eat almonds.' Women, according to the study, were another big draw. Paramjit Singh Judge, one of the authors of this study, asserts, 'I know one doctor in Majitha who terminated 10-15 pregnancies every Thursday. No one openly told you of the rapes. But in the villages, you often heard comments like, "*Itna badaam khayenge to kahin to nikalenge hi.*" [If they eat so many almonds, they have to

find an outlet for their energies]. Often terrorists would enter a house
just before dinner, have dinner, and then force all the family members
except the young women up to the terrace . . . The majority of the
terrorists died within a year. In that time they had access to 50 to 55
women.'

Yet the conventional stereotypes of terrorists – noble freedom
fighters or unhinged fanatics – persist. Part of the problem, at least,
is a question of focus. The act of terror – with its extraordinary drama
– naturally attracts overwhelming attention, and lends itself easily to
unidimensional exaggeration. But terrorism as opposed to a terrorist
incident is a far more complex phenomenon. It involves structures
and functions that are often altogether divorced from this macabre
theatre of blood. Terrorist organisations – and especially those that
have attained a certain minimal scale of operations – engage in a
wide range of activities: ideology building and projection; political
and cadre mobilisation; recruitment; fund raising and financial
management; the co-ordination of overground political, financial and
legal activities in support of their movements; cadre management and
internal conflict resolution; discipline and the infliction of punishment
on recalcitrant cadres, as well as competing groupings; training;
weapons procurement; the management of non-military supplies and
logistics; the setting up of training camps and the conduct of training
courses; intelligence gathering and communications, to name a few.
It is more than evident that the men who carry out these widely
varied activities cannot fall into a single and rigid stereotype of the
terrorist personality.

The profiling of terrorists – both prominent leaders and lesser
cadres – assumes great significance within this context. If carried out
with intelligence and sensitivity, such profiling can produce a nuanced
picture of the complex realities of terrorism, and can help understand
patterns of mobilisation for extremist enterprises. They can, equally,
help understand what happens in democratic societies when they are
confronted with violence of this type, and the degree to which they
fail to comprehend the dangers to which their very fundamental
structures, institutions and processes are exposed. Democratic polities
have tended to go along with the stock explanations of political
violence and have often been misled into responses that encourage
and consolidate terrorist movements, at least in the initial stages, and
to the point when these become entrenched and relatively intractable.

Within democracies, moreover, it is essential to understand the
peculiar appeal of terrorist leaders and movements, and the pattern

of support they generate. There is, at present, little awareness of the complex dynamics of extremist mass mobilisation, and the combination of charismatic and coercive methods it employs. Indeed, confusion over the nature of this support has resulted in a great crisis of confidence within democratic communities and institutions, who often and mistakenly come to regard terrorist movements as if they were inchoate expressions of popular democratic sentiments, instead of what they actually are: the fundamental and complete negation of what democracy seeks and represents.

Thus, again and again, influential liberal democrats drawn from a range of professions – prominently politicians, lawyers, judges, human rights activists and journalists – argue against the use of legitimate force in counter-terrorism, appealing, instead, for a directionless battle for the hearts and minds of the misguided youth. This is not a failing unique to democrats in India. Indeed, there has been a general, albeit implicit, assumption of popular support to terrorist movements in most theatres of conflict in the world far in excess of what actually exists on the ground or among the societies on whose behalf the terrorists claim to speak. Such assumptions are apparently ratified by the public statements of many leaders and even of the 'common people' and the local media, from time to time. And yet, they are utterly false – though this fact can only be confirmed after the terror has been conclusively defeated. This is precisely what happened in Punjab of the 1980s. At the end, I recall many a muddle-headed liberal arguing that we had lost the hearts and minds of the people of Punjab, and so there was little sense in holding on to a piece of land. Thousands, at times even hundreds of thousands, assembled at prayer ceremonies of slain terrorists, and the media pointed to this as intractable evidence of the mass support that the Khalistanis enjoyed. But by 1992, when the terrorists were in open flight, there was visible elation in the streets as markets began to remain open late into the evenings, and I recall the sheer jubilation that marked the first musical night – organised by the Punjab police at Tarn Taran in what had been the terrorist heartland – that was attended by thousands of people rediscovering their freedom. Again, those who pointed to the low voter turnout in the assembly elections of February 1992 as evidence of popular alienation had no explanation for the over 75 per cent voter turnout in the elections to 95 municipal committees just six months later; and a voter turnout of 82 per cent when Panchayat elections were held in 12,342 villages in January 1993. The fact is there can be no real assessment of the popular will in the shadow of terrorist violence.

This was the principle that was reiterated in the jubilation that was expressed by a free Afghan people after the rout of the Taliban. It is possible to discover, once again, in this recent experience, the anatomy of a terrorised society. Right to the end of the US-Northern Alliance-Eastern Alliance campaigns in Afghanistan, we discovered only three pockets of serious Taliban resistance – Kunduz, Kandahar and Tora Bora. Estimates of total Taliban forces in these locations stood at about 30,000. Even among these, the Afghans themselves – numerically the largest component of these forces – were far from committed to the extremist vision, and showed themselves not only willing, but eager to arrive at a settlement with the new powers in the war ravaged nation (as, indeed, they did eight years earlier, in the face of the Pakistan-backed sweep of the Taliban across their country). The only elements of serious resistance were, in fact, the foreign terrorists – the Arabs, the Pakistanis, the Chechens, the Algerians, the Fillipinos, and the smattering of other nationalities among the 'lunatics of Allah' who were actually willing to die for their 'cause' – and at least part of their 'commitment', in these last engagements, would be the result of their fear of reprisals and the repeated assertion by Afghanistan's new leaders that, while Afghan Taliban could be forgiven and accommodated, the foreigners would be mistaken if they expected clemency.

It was overwhelmingly evident, moreover, that the defeat and the flight of the Taliban was greeted with unconstrained delight by the mass of people in Afghanistan. How, then, is it that a few thousand foreign fanatics and mercenaries, backed by a small number of no more than compliant locals, could enslave a nation of 26 million for nearly eight years of unrelieved suffering? A nation, moreover, that is celebrated for its proud, combative, unyielding and warlike people?

The truth is, the impact of the introduction of sophisticated and extremely lethal weaponry, in the hands of people who have no qualms in using it ruthlessly against unarmed civilians – including women and children – for the purposes of creating terror cannot even be imagined except by those who have actually experienced it. It is nonsense to talk about the will of the people under the shadow of the gun. There is, in fact, a societal Stockholm Syndrome, a pattern of resignation, submission, acceptance and eventual justification that becomes a necessary survival strategy under extreme, lawless and pervasive threat.

Terrorism – even by small but well-armed, and especially externally supported groups – has the capacity to produce, in large masses of men, a widespread belief in the futility of resistance and a loss of faith in the state and its agencies and their ability to protect life, liberty and property. These patterns of thought gradually create a denial among the people of their own fear, and an increasing justification of, and identification with, the terrorist cause. However outrageous the extremist demands may be, the logic of these demands begins to find sympathetic echoes among the people, the media and the secular or moderate leadership as well. Gradually, this is also translated into an increasing willingness to provide, at least, non-terrorist support to the activities of the terrorists – feeding, harbouring, sympathetic *bandhs*, *dharnas* and protests, the creation and operation of front organisations that take up the cause of the human rights of arrested terrorists, etc. To believe that these are the acts of a free people, willingly undertaken, is to utterly and completely misunderstand the very nature of terrorism. Indeed, the most tragic, the most pathetic symbols of terrorism are not the mutilated corpses that are so often projected through the media, but the images of members of the Dukhtaran-e-Millat (Daughters of Islam) singing paeans to their own enslavement, or of the homage that the Hurriyat pays, from time to time, to the *mehmaan mujahiddeen*, the guest militants, and to Pakistan, whose ambitions and machinations kill thousands of innocent Kashmiris every year.

There is an important lesson here that is only slowly being realised: political solutions must not, of course, be abandoned in situations of widespread terrorist conflict. But where terrorists and their front organisations have occupied the entire political space, it is both wrong and suicidal for democracies to seek such a negotiated solution with mass murderers, with their overground representatives, or with their state sponsors. Political solutions in a democracy can only be pursued with those political actors who are untainted by associations with terrorism. As for those who practice or support terrorism – the response can only be that of confrontation with the fullest might of the state. As Fareed Zakaria has noted in another context, 'Military victory is indeed essential. Radical political Islam is an "armed doctrine", in Edmund Burke's phrase. Like other armed doctrines before it – fascism, for example – it can be discredited only by first being defeated.'

This also raises the pressing issue of the increasing use of religion – or more correctly, religious identity – as against the political ideologies of the past, as the primary source and justification for terrorism across the world. Institutionalised religions have, of course, been a major mobilising instrumentality throughout history for political actions of the most extreme kind – including, for example, wars, genocidal sectarian pogroms, mass communal rioting, terrorism and, within the Indian subcontinent, the indiscriminate excesses of Partition in 1947. The revival of this instrument in an overwhelming proportion of violent and extremist movements across the world, and in widely disparate social, economic and political circumstances, is a matter of great concern, and, after decades of a growing faith in 'enlightenment values', particularly democratic liberalism, a matter of some surprise and incomprehension. There is an enormous need, today, to break down this pattern of mass mobilisation into its components and, in view of the sweeping demonisation of entire faiths because of the actions of some of their members, to secure a clear separation between the actual tenets of the faith in question, the practices and beliefs of the larger mass of its followers, and the distortions or interpretations that lend themselves to extremist and terrorist movements. While speaking to many arrested terrorists in Punjab I found that, though the Khalistani ideology was supposed to be based on the Sikh scriptures, their knowledge of these scriptures was uniformly rudimentary, and in some cases, non-existent. Some of the terrorist leaders could not even recite a single stanza from the *Granth Sahib*, the Sikh holy book, and were ignorant of the basic tenets of Sikhism. And yet, the intensity of the conviction with which they sought to inflict their belief systems and their codes of conduct on others through extreme violence was difficult to imagine.

There are parallels here with what has been seen in the idiosyncratic religious despotism that Mullah Omar established in Afghanistan under the rule of the Taliban. It is interesting to note that 'Mullah' Omar was, in fact, a drop-out from a religious seminary, and evidently lacked the application and perhaps intelligence to complete the course of study that would have qualified him for the title he pretended to. And yet, an entire nation became victim to his religious bigotry.

The essence of this bigotry is not, as its proponents and apologists often project, a core of fundamental religious beliefs and practices. It is, in fact, the construction of a hated 'Other'. Bhindranwale attributed all the supposed suffering of the Sikh community to the evil Brahmins who ruled from Delhi, and ascribed to the Hindus at large both a power and a malignancy that were entirely of his own imagining. This was combined with extreme doctrinal simplification of selective passages derived from the Sikh scriptures and history to justify violence against the hated Other. Once again, the recent televised speeches of Osama bin Laden, with their boundless hatred for America and the West, exemplify the fact that religious identity, here, is defined, not by a positive vision of humanity based on the scriptures, but through a process of exclusion of and contrast against the hated Other.

There are, clearly, many unresolved issues relating to the psychology of terrorism – both regarding those who initiate and participate in these movements, as well as those, including entire communities and societies, that are its direct or indirect victims. There is a growing, albeit fragmentary body, of literature on various aspects of this subject sourced particularly from the West, and it is now increasingly realised that, in order to understand terrorist motivations there must be a greater focus on the protracted process of indoctrination that terrorists go through, and a shift of attention from personality to process. With the enormous concentration of terrorism in the South Asian region, it is now crucial that these processes be documented and analysed, both for movements that have been defeated, and those that are yet to be brought to an end.

'If the instigation for
jihad against the
Americans and Israelis
to liberate the Al-Aqsa
mosque and Holy Ka'aba
is considered a crime, let
history be witness that I
am a criminal.'

Osama bin Laden: Al Qaeda

Rahimullah Yusufzai

The day after he survived a US cruise missile attack on his camp in Khost, southern Afghanistan, I received a satellite phone call from Osama bin Laden. On the line was his friend, political adviser and, some say, organisational brain, Dr Ayman Al-Zawahiri. 'Mr bin Laden is sitting beside me,' Al-Zawahiri said. 'As he cannot speak English he asked me to convey to you that we have survived the American missile attack. Tell the Americans that the war has just begun. They should now wait for the answer.'

The answer, it now appears, came three years later when 11 September 2001 made a ghastly hole through which the US viewed, very differently, the menace of terrorism. What was a distant threat somewhere else became a horrific reality at home. The US retaliated by bombing Afghanistan, targetting the Taliban and their guest, bin Laden. The terrorist camps in Afghanistan run by the man accused of being the jihad paymaster were the prime target of its military campaign that began on 7 October 2001.

Bin Laden was not an unknown enemy for the US though. Just an extraordinarily difficult one who could not be sighted, maimed or killed even with a 25 million dollar reward on his head. As early as 1998, President Bill Clinton had described him as America's public enemy number one after US embassies in Nairobi, Kenya, and Dar es Salam, Tanzania, had been bombed. Then, the Americans had struck. They sent 80 Tomahawk cruise missiles over Pakistani airspace to hit bin Laden's training camps in Khost – to no effect. Contrary to US intelligence reports, bin Laden was not in the camp and no big meeting of his followers belonging to Al Qaeda or The Base – a secretive organisation working for global Islamist goals – was scheduled that night.

This encounter established the pattern for later ones. The US would use superior firepower against an adversary holed up in inaccessible terrain; there would be no direct engagement; and credible intelligence would be hard to come by. Result: US strikes would bloody the waters but not catch the big fish.

The adversary, on the other hand, would train guns through the media. Indeed, the Americans sighted the adversary only on the television screen, through video messages spouting anti-West rhetoric. Bin Laden became a significant presence in the American drawing room only in 1998 when the Western media sought his interviews and CNN and ABC crews travelled to Jalalabad to talk to him.

Bin Laden, a deft media manipulator, would always talk tough in such interviews. It emerged in these media sessions that his foremost priority was to force the US, British and French troops to quit Saudi Arabia both for patriotic and Islamic reasons. He saw them as occupation troops sent to protect the West's oil interests and sustain the 'corrupt, unrepresentative and pro-West' Saudi royal family in power. He insisted that 'infidels' were not allowed to set foot in or near Islam's two holiest places, Makkah and Madina. He cited the two bombings of US army barracks in Saudi Arabia in the mid-1990s as indicators of strong opposition to their presence in his native country. He warned that more such attacks would follow until the foreign soldiers, mostly Americans, were made to leave.

Bin Laden's appearance does not support such hard talk. The world's most wanted terrorist comes across as modest and polite, serene and soft spoken. His hands are as soft as a multimillionaire who has never known hard labour. He is charismatic and somewhat shy. The only visible sign that lends ferocity to his otherwise gentle appearance is his AK-47 (Kalashnikov), which he carries all the time. His men are keen to narrate how he snatched it from a Soviet soldier in hand-to-hand combat during the Afghan jihad.

If appearances are deceptive, then precise information about Osama ('the lion') bin Mohammad bin Awad bin Laden's early life is difficult to obtain in the absence of an authentic biography. Born in 1957 in the Saudi Arabian capital, Riyadh, bin Laden was raised in Madina and Jeddah, where he received his school education. He studied management and economics at the King Abdul Aziz University, Jeddah. He was one of 54 children of Mohammad bin Laden, a man of Yemeni origin. His mother, Aalia, was a Syrian from Jabaryoun village and the last of his father's four official wives. The mother and son had a strong relationship because he was her only child. His father left Yemen where he was a porter in the port of Aden to try his luck in Saudi Arabia. Having befriended the kingdom's founder, Abdul Aziz al Saud, Mohammad bin Laden won government contracts and founded a construction company that made him one of Saudi Arabia's wealthiest men. The firm, now a respected name in Saudi Arabia with assets worth $ 5 billion, carried out construction works in Makkah and Madina and renovated Prophet Mohammad's mosque, leaving a deep impact on the young bin Laden. His father died in a helicopter crash in 1968.

Bin Laden inherited a small fortune while still in his teens. At 19, he married his Syrian cousin, Naji, who was only 13. She was the first of his four wives and the mother of his favourite son, Abdullah. The number of his children is said to be two dozen.

Most accounts agree that bin Laden had a religious bent of mind from his youth and was regular in his prayers as compared to other teenagers. His contacts with members of the Muslim Brotherhood, an Islamic movement that originated in Egypt, also influenced his thinking. One of his teachers at the King Abdul Aziz University in Jeddah was Dr Sheikh Abdullah Azzam, a Palestinian-Jordanian who moved to Peshawar after the Soviet invasion of Afghanistan in December 1979 and started inviting and organising Arab nationals to take part in the Afghan war. Bin Laden later teamed up with Azzam to set up an office, Maktab Al-Khidmat, in Peshawar to serve Arab volunteers entering and coming out of Afghanistan. He also helped establish a camp in Sadda, in Pakistan's tribal area, Kurram Agency, to impart military training to Arabs and set up the Ma'sadad Al-Ansar base in Afghanistan to fight the Soviet Red Army and Afghan communists. Bin Laden is said to have fought in the battles for Khost, Jaji and Jalalabad along with his Arab colleagues.

The Soviet military intervention had the most profound

influence on bin Laden, prompting the 22-year-old to reputedly place his considerable wealth at the disposal of the Afghan mujahideen, widows and orphans. In his interviews, bin Laden told of how he transferred heavy construction equipment including bulldozers, loaders, and dump trucks from Saudi Arabia to Afghanistan for building roads, boring tunnels to store arms and ammunition, digging trenches and setting up hospitals. He spoke about the immense spiritual benefit he obtained from his participation in the Afghan jihad and explained how it enabled the Muslims to destroy the myth of the invincibility of one superpower (the former Soviet Union) and prepared them to confront the might of the remaining one (US). 'Today, the entire Muslim world, by the grace of God, has imbibed the faithful spirit of strength and started to interact in a good manner to end occupation and the Western and American influence on our countries,' he once said.

Religion occupies a large part of his discourse. But bin Laden is also an intelligent man who can be witty at times. During an interview I asked him how many children he had. There was a burst of laughter when he replied: 'I have lost count!' Was he still a multimillionaire and how much was his worth? Before I had finished my question, bin Laden had put his hand on his heart and said: 'I am Ghani (rich) here.' And when I asked him how he could challenge the world's only superpower operating out of a poor, war-ravaged country like Afghanistan, bin Laden looked up to the skies, raised his index finger, and replied that there was only one real superpower and that was God Almighty.

Fed up with mujahideen infighting in Afghanistan after Soviet withdrawal in February 1989, bin Laden returned home to Saudi Arabia where he was received as a national hero. For some time everything went well. There were reports that bin Laden was organising men to fight the Marxist regime in South Yemen. Then Iraq invaded Kuwait on 2 August 1990 and the Saudi government thought of inviting US troops to repel the invaders. Bin Laden offered to raise a force of 100,000 volunteers to defend Saudi Arabia and evict Iraq from Kuwait. His proposal was rejected and he felt humiliated. Further, Operation Desert Storm saw the US despatch troops and planes to Saudi Arabia to the utter disgust of bin Laden who detested the idea of armed non-Muslims treading holy ground. This stand put bin Laden in the camp of the Saudi dissidents. Things came to a head when bin Laden publicly opposed the Saudi government's decision to invite US forces. His passport was taken away to stop him from travelling outside Saudi Arabia but he was allowed to go abroad when he offered to fly to Afghanistan to mediate between the warring Afghan factions. However, he travelled to Pakistan and a group of Saudi dissidents formed around him. Together, they launched their anti-Saudi campaign.

At around this time, Sudan was ruled by an Islamic coalition, the National Islamic Front (NIF), led by President General Omar Al-Bashir and Dr Hassan Al-Turabi, a Sorbonne-educated cleric.

Al-Turabi believed the US could be taken on and defeated by the Islamists. He invited bin Laden and Al Qaeda to Sudan and bin Laden decided to shift operations there. His authority in Pakistan had already been eroded after Benazir Bhutto's government had survived a no-confidence motion he had funded. Besides, the Al Qaeda were getting restless.

Bin Laden found Sudan to his liking. The government was friendly and many Islamists and revolutionaries like him had taken refuge in the country. He dressed like the Sudanese, won government contracts to build roads, started an import and export business and bought land for farming. He set up nearly 30 firms in Sudan while Al Qaeda worked with Sudan intelligence. In exchange, the NIF gave the Al Qaeda land for training camps. Bin Laden cultivated the government ministers and department bosses. He also bred horses, a passion that he tried to continue even in Afghanistan.

From Sudan, bin Laden networked with several groups and set up links with offices in London, New York and Turkey. Al Qaeda drew on a floating group of veteran Arab mujahideen who were evading arrest from their own regimes. Bin Laden's organisation, with its financial and infrastructural resources in Sudan, proved an ideal refuge, retraining the mujahideen and re-fanning the fires of jihad.

By this time, the US and Egypt had begun pestering the Sudanese government to expel him. Bin Laden was gaining a reputation as a jihad paymaster and was being blamed for terrorist attacks in Egypt, Saudi Arabia and the US. The Saudi government stripped him of citizenship in 1994 and forced his family to disown him. This was the beginning of an open confrontation between bin Laden and the Saudi royal family. He retaliated by forming an opposition group called the Advice and Reform Committee. In late 1995, bin Laden's house in a Khartoum suburb was fired at by a group of gunmen, two of whom died along with four bin Laden men. The next year, bin Laden was finally asked to leave Sudan following an assassination attempt on President Mubarak by an Egyptian group linked to him and in the wake of truck bombings at US bases in Saudi Arabia. The Sudanese government could no longer host bin Laden as there was growing pressure from the US and Egypt. And he could think of no other place than Afghanistan to give him refuge.

The mujahideen-ruled Afghanistan welcomed him with open arms when he flew to Jalalabad, eastern Afghanistan, on 18 May 1996 on a chartered plane with his family and supporters. First the mujahideen and subsequently the Taliban treated him as a guest, upholding the tradition of Afghan hospitality. Mujahideen commander Engineer Mahmood and Hezb-i-Islami leader Maulvi Yunis Khalis, whom he knew from the days of the Afghan jihad, helped him resume life in Afghanistan. He put up his men in the Tora Bora camp while his family took up residence in a new residential area near Jalalabad. Khalis was one of his neighbours and firm supporters.

Bin Laden was in Jalalabad when the city fell to the Taliban on 12 September 1996. Subsequently on 27 September, the Taliban captured Kabul after driving out the then President Burhanuddin Rabbani and his Defence Minister Ahmad Shah Masood. Initially, the Taliban distrusted bin Laden because they thought the Saudi-born militant and multimillionaire had until then backed Rabbani and Masood. It took a few meetings between bin Laden and Taliban emissary Mulla Mohammad Sadiq to remove these misgivings. Later, the Taliban asked bin Laden to shift to Kandahar, the spiritual capital of the Taliban Islamic Movement and the headquarters of their supreme leader, Mulla Mohammad Omar. Bin Laden's four wives and several children lived in Kandahar until the US attacks forced them to shift to the countryside. As for bin Laden, he kept shifting places all these years and lived at one of his over half a dozen hideouts, including Khost. Other hideouts prior to 11 September were near Kandahar and in Urozgan, Nimruz, Logar, Kabul and Nangarhar provinces.

Soon Mulla Omar could be heard complaining that bin Laden's criticism of the US, Saudi Arabia and other countries had cost his isolated regime its few remaining friends. This was partly due to bin Laden's penchant for publicity. So keen was he to send across his message to the world, despite his natural shyness, that he appeared willing to grant media interviews on a daily basis.

His first interview on returning to Afghanistan, after five and a half years in the Sudan and making significant investments there, was with Robert Fisk of *The Independent* in 1996. In the interview, he demanded the pullout of the US, British and French troops from Saudi Arabia. Two years later, he was far more strident. He held a press conference for Pakistani journalists in Khost on 25 May 1998 to announce the launching of the International Islamic Front for Jihad against the Christians and Jews (or against the US and Israel, as he explained).

But the news conference had been held without the permission of Mulla Omar, who was furious. The Mulla warned that Afghanistan could have only one ruler – either him or his Saudi guest. Mulla Omar, who controlled access to bin Laden, did not want him to create problems for the Taliban through his frequent outbursts. Bin Laden was later summoned to Kandahar and plainly told by Omar not to test the limits of Taliban hospitality. Subsequently, bin Laden had to issue a statement declaring his acceptance of Omar as Afghanistan's Amirul Momineen (Commander of the Faithful) and pledging unconditional support to the Taliban's policies. Around this time, the Taliban also claimed to have restricted bin Laden's access to the world, monitoring and curtailing his movements and taking away his satellite phone and fax machine.

When this writer met bin Laden for the second time, on 23 December 1998, at his makeshift tented camp in a desert near Kandahar, he complained that the Taliban had turned down repeated requests to invite me to interview him. His lieutenants –

speaking through the English-speaking Dr Ayman Al-Zawahiri, leader of the radical Egyptian Al-Jihad (Islamic Jihad) group – argued that the Taliban should allow bin Laden more access to the press. Now that he is being accused of committing every act of terrorism taking place, they said, he could clarify his position and explain his mission.

Much has also been written about the growing influence of bin Laden on the Taliban. At first, bin Laden and his Arab supporters, who numbered less than 1,000 before the US started its aerial strikes in Afghanistan, depended on the Taliban for almost everything, including security and housing. They could not afford to offend the Taliban, especially Mulla Omar. No country was willing to give them refuge and none of them could return to their respective Arab countries because all of them were wanted.

Secondly, the Taliban policies on the Buddha statues in Bamiyan and Western NGOs, were shaped by hardline elements in the Taliban movement led by Mulla Omar; not by bin Laden and his Arabs. The fact is that the Taliban fighters had tried to destroy the giant Buddhas in 1997 immediately after conquering Bamiyan but could not as they lacked the required explosives. At that stage, bin Laden had not been declared America's public enemy number one and was not attracting media attention. So there were no suggestions then that he had hijacked the Taliban regime and was responsible for the hardening of Taliban policies. It was, in fact, the UN Security Council sanctions against Afghanistan, delivered as a punishment for refusing to deliver bin Laden to face trial on terrorism charges and the non-recognition of the Taliban regime by the UN and the West, that made the Taliban angry and inflexible.

In retaliation, the Taliban destroyed the Bamiyan Buddhas despite pleas by the international community, including friends such as Pakistan and foes like the US. It also boycotted the UN peace mission for Afghanistan and acted tough with regard to the arrest and trial of eight aid workers from Germany, the US and Australia who had been accused of preaching Christianity.

Of course, there is no denying that the Arab volunteers who came to fight in Afghanistan during the Afghan jihad were fanatically anti-West. There were numerous incidents when Arab fighters threatened Western journalists covering the Afghan war. They also killed some Afghan soldiers taken prisoner for fighting for Kabul's communist regime. The Arab fighters also used to force some of their Afghan mujahideen colleagues during the war against the Soviets in Afghanistan to pray regularly and to grow beards.

When it came to bin Laden, the Taliban earned both praise and criticism for their handling of the issue. Many were impressed with their conduct, which they saw as following the best traditions of the Afghan people, when they hosted a man who had sought protection in Afghanistan after falling on bad times. Critics, on the other hand, argued that the Taliban stand on bin Laden inflicted suffering on their people and brought their war-ravaged country to the brink of another war.

What actually worked for bin Laden was the nearly mythical role attributed to him. How successful has this been! Famous people have tried to score political points by exploiting the notoriety associated with bin Laden. Russia's Mikhail Gorbachev claimed bin Laden tried to have him killed; Pakistan's Benazir Bhutto alleged bin Laden gave money to politicians to oust her from power as prime minister during an Opposition no-trust move in the Pakistani parliament and Indian politician Jayalalitha accused him of destabilising her Tamil Nadu state in south India by sponsoring bomb explosions and militant groups. The fact is he is often misrepresented. For one, the authenticity of some of the videotapes attributed to him has not been established. Sometimes, old footage is put together to sell to television firms eager to lay their hands on anything concerning bin Laden. Besides, those claiming to speak on his behalf need to be checked for credibility. In the past, a person who claimed bin Laden had declared jihad against India and appointed him as his military commander in Indian Kashmir turned out to be a liar. Also, intelligence agencies all over the world have found it convenient to blame him as a scapegoat to hide their own shortcomings.

The effect? Bin Laden has gained something of a cult status in the Islamic world: the more he is targetted by the US; the more he becomes a hero in the eyes of most practicing Muslims. Parents in growing numbers in parts of Afghanistan and Pakistan have named their sons Osama, a rare name in this part of the world. His admirers say they are impressed by his courage in challenging the world's only superpower at a time when even nuclear countries such as Pakistan cannot stand up to the US. His posters and T-shirts, marketed by enterprising business persons, sell well.

It is not that he has no opponents in Pakistan or in neighbouring Afghanistan. Many Pakistanis and Afghans, more so those who are liberal, secular and leftist, blame him for bringing suffering on the Afghans and using violence to achieve his objectives. The truth would lie between the two extremes.

The real bin Laden is frail and ill. His right-hand man, Al-Zawahiri, was willing to share some, but not all, information about bin Laden's health. Bin Laden's permanent backache is no longer a secret, forcing him to walk with the help of a cane. During an interview, his aides politely erased footage of bin Laden walking with a stick in hand from my digital camera and forbade me from filming until he sat down. They were obviously concerned that bin Laden's image as a fearless man would suffer if he was shown in a state of physical vulnerability. He also suffers from a kidney ailment and low blood pressure. There were reports of an Iraqi doctor having gone to Afghanistan to treat his kidney. He was once seen being taken to a hospital in Kabul for kidney dialysis. As Pakistan's President General Pervez Musharraf disclosed, bin Laden arranged for two dialysis machines to be delivered to him in Afghanistan for his treatment. However, reports of his marriage to a young girl from Yemen, which were again never confirmed, prompted his admirers to say that he was not ill.

One has to take these reports with a pinch of salt. Bin Laden loves to talk big and is always ready to make use of the media to create an impact. As part of his self-promotion, he reportedly hired an Egyptian journalist during the early years of his life in Afghanistan to record his and his group's exploits. An incident during this writer's visit to his camp in Khost province in May 1998 – when he gave his well-known press conference – also bears this out. Smuggled across Pakistan's mountainous border with Afghanistan by the pro-bin Laden militant Islamic group, Harkat-ul-Ansar, our group of 14 Pakistani journalists was kept waiting for three days after being promised a meeting with the man himself. Before our patience could run out, we were packed into sturdy Toyota pick-up trucks and driven across harsh terrain on a non-existent road. Five hours later, we found ourselves in a camp largely made of mud houses. I instantly recognised it from my earlier visits. It emerged that this camp was only half-an-hour's drive from where we spent three days and nights waiting for the interview. The long wait and the backbreaking journey were evidently meant to show us that bin Laden's camp was remote and inaccessible.

There was more to come once we arrived at the camp, barricaded by a barbed wire and teeming with armed men. Bin Laden, his pick-up truck leading a convoy of vehicles, made a grand entry. As he disembarked, surrounded by about 20 hooded bodyguards, the sleepy valley suddenly came alive with gunfire. Gunmen deployed on mountain peaks fired their Russian-made Zikoyak and Dachaka heavy machineguns and rocket-launchers into the air to light up the dark sky. The celebratory firing continued for the next 15 minutes or so as bin Laden, visible from afar due to his six feet-plus height, walked slowly towards us and into the large room where he was scheduled to hold the press meet. It was an impressive show of firepower and some of us were overawed.

However, my language skills soon enabled me to find out from the Pashto-speaking gunmen that they were not bin Laden's men and had been invited to put up the show for the visiting journalists. Among them were Afghans and Pakistanis receiving military training at the complex of six camps in the area and all were asked to bring their own guns for the purpose. As a result, for the uninitiated in our group, bin Laden emerged as a powerful military commander after stage-managing this fierce public display of firepower.

Bin Laden's skills are seen best in his video messages in which he comes across as a shrewd man who is able to keep the US government guessing about his intentions and whereabouts. Just when speculation was rife that he could have been killed in the two-week long US bombings in the Tora Bora area in Spinghar mountains, bin Laden stunned the world by producing yet another tape with the same anti-West message that has become his life's mission. His calmness and defiance in the tape were surprising for a man being tracked down by the world's only superpower with all the might and resources at its command. The video showed that bin Laden had not lost his nerves despite the fall of the Taliban regime that gave him protection.

If bin Laden were to be believed, the tape was recorded three months after the September 11 attacks in the US and two months following the start of American aerial strikes in Afghanistan. That means it was recorded between the first and second week of December 2001. It seems the recording was done when bin Laden's Tora Bora cave hideouts near Jalalabad came under intense bombing by US warplanes and a ground offensive by Afghan fighters loyal to three Eastern Shura military commanders. What happened to bin Laden after the tape was produced would most likely give many more sleepless nights to American intelligence.

This was the third bin Laden video in three months. All were cleverly timed for release. The first was made available to Qatar's Al-Jazeera television on 7 October 2001, the day the US started aerial strikes in Taliban-ruled Afghanistan, and telecast the same night. It got prime-time television coverage all over the world and contributed towards the monopoly enjoyed by the US media networks. The second tape, again supplied to the Arabic language Al-Jazeera, was telecast on 3 November 2001. The third tape came at a time when the US military campaign in Afghanistan was said to be in its final stages. The message sent by bin Laden suggested otherwise because the campaign would not be over until the US achieves its primary aim which, in the words of US President George W. Bush, is to get bin Laden 'dead or alive'.

A comparison of the three tapes shows that bin Laden's beard has greyed considerably since 7 October. It seems his tough life in harsh surroundings and his constant struggle to avoid arrest has taken its toll. But it has not broken his spirit as evidenced in his defiance of the US and the West. Unlike the last two videos that were recorded with rocks in the background, bin Laden has chosen a different setting for the third tape. He was obviously aware that American geologists would figure out his location in Afghanistan by studying the rocks seen in the background. So, this time a blanket seems to have been placed in the background to disguise the shooting location of the 33-minute tape. Bin Laden used to have some cameras and recording equipment and a few trained men who could produce homemade videos. The apparatus and those who operate it are obviously still able to function despite the US military campaign in Afghanistan. That bin Laden was able to supply these tapes to Al-Jazeera's offices first in Kabul and now in Pakistan shows that his loyal messengers are still operational and so more such tapes can be expected to surface in the months ahead. As for the contents of bin Laden's message in his latest tape, it was a shrewd effort to mobilise Muslim public opinion against the US and the West.

Bin Laden would not have landed in trouble if he didn't have the habit of talking big. By declaring jihad on the United States and Israel, he ensured that he would be the prime suspect in any act of terrorism targeting the Americans. This has happened in the past and was the case again on 11 September. Even before the collapse of the World Trade Center towers following the attack, accusing fingers were being pointed at bin Laden and Al Qaeda.

A scrutiny of Al Qaeda also gives the lie to bin Laden's larger-than-life image. Al Qaeda is small and loosely knit. It is a member of the International Islamic Front for Jihad against the US and Israel that was supposed to serve as an umbrella organisation for Islamic groups worldwide. Only a few groups, mostly led by Arabs based in Afghanistan, have joined it. Among them are Dr Al-Zawahiri's Al-Jihad from Egypt and Sheikh Omar Abdur Rahman's Al Jamaah Al Islamiah (Islamic Group), another Egyptian organisation. The Sheikh is the blind Egyptian preacher who is now in a US jail following his conviction in the 1993 bombing of the World Trade Center. His two young sons are in Afghanistan and are lieutenants of bin Laden. Some Algerians, Moroccans and Libyans are also members of the Front.

Though they broadly agree on the need to jointly fight against US and Western hegemony and to strive for Islam's glory, all the groups and individuals have their own political and military agendas. They all aim to bring Islamic revolutions in their respective countries. Thus, the Egyptians are fighting to oust President Hosni Mubarak from power and replace him with the Islamists. The Algerians want an Islamic government in their country. Islamic groups from Pakistan, the Philippines and certain other countries may be in agreement with the objectives of bin Laden's Front but they do not say publicly that they are its members or are working for its aims. Some of the groups and individuals had also signed the fatwa (religious decree) taken out by bin Laden to justify jihad against the US and Israel.

Bin Laden's strength was due a great deal to the men who work with him. They were seldom mentioned because all attention was focused on him. Important in their own right, they were fugitives from the law in their native Arab countries or wanted by the United States on terrorism charges. Together they ran Al Qaeda.

The most prominent Al Qaeda leaders after bin Laden were Al-Zawahiri and Sheikh Taseer Abdullah. The doctor was often referred to as the brain of the organisation while the Sheikh was its military commander. Both were from Egypt and were veterans of the Afghan jihad against the Soviet occupation troops during 1979-89. Another prominent bin Laden associate was Shawki Al-Islambouli, a brother of Khalid Al-Islambouli who shot dead Egyptian President Anwar Sadat during a military parade in Cairo 20 years ago.

It is surprising that almost all top-ranked Al Qaeda leaders, except bin Laden, were Egyptians. It may be interpreted as proof of the success achieved by Egypt's President Mubarak in ruthlessly driving out most of his Islamist opponents from the country. Or is it that the exiled Egyptian Islamists are more organised in Taliban-ruled Afghanistan and are, therefore, able to monopolise the Al Qaeda hierarchy?

Al-Zawahiri is a 50-year-old physician and probably the most learned among bin Laden's associates. He is a short, stocky man. His grandfather was well-known as the mufti of Cairo's Al-Azhar University, one of the most respected centres of Islamic learning in the world. His father was his country's ambassador in Pakistan in the 1950s. The bespectacled and bearded Al-Zawahiri is a feared man in Egypt and the country's security agencies consider his followers more radical than other Islamists. He was the leader of the Al-Jihad group, which took credit for the 1981 assassination of Egyptian President Anwar Sadat. Fluent in English, he often serves as an interpreter for bin Laden.

Al-Zawahiri, comfortably dressed in the Afghan *shalwar-kameez* and turban, came across as a knowledgeable man who kept himself abreast of the world. He said his wife and children, now believed to be dead in the US bombing, willingly shared hardships with him in Afghanistan for almost two decades because they considered the shift from Egypt to Afghanistan a *hijrat* (migration) in Allah's cause. He was hoping to forge an alliance with other Islamic forces in Egypt, in particular with Al Jamaah Al Islamiah led by Sheikh Omar Abdul Rahman. Together, he wanted his Al-Jihad, or Islamic Jihad, and other Islamic groups to oust the dictatorial, pro-West Mubarak government and Islamise Egypt. He had no doubt that Egypt's Islamic groups would triumph eventually though he could not say when and how it would happen.

It was through Al-Zawahiri that one was able to piece together a picture of the life of bin Laden and his friends. Bin Laden, Al-Zawahiri and Sheikh Taseer Abdullah almost always stayed together, consulted each other and maintained family ties. Bin Laden's eldest son, Mohammad, married Abdullah's daughter in February 2001. Videotapes of the wedding were sent out to a select group of Afghan, Pakistani and Arab Islamist politicians, journalists and academics. They showed the garlanded bridegroom sitting between his father and father-in-law while bin Laden made a stirring pro-Intifada speech in support of the Palestinians and against the Israelis.

Along with bin Laden and others, Al-Zawahiri was indicted by a US court in the 1998 bombings of the American embassies in Kenya and Tanzania that killed 240 people, including 12 Americans. The Interpol issued an international warrant of arrest against Al-Zawahiri. But the US government has yet to announce a reward for his capture. This makes him less dangerous, in theory, than Abdullah, for whose capture Washington had promised to pay $ 5 million. Described as Mohammad Atef in US government records, Abdullah's nom de guerre is Abu Hafs Al-Misri. It is taken from the name of his first-born son, a practice followed by most Arabs. The US government believes he is the military commander of Al Qaeda. In his own words, Abdullah said he was bin Laden's security chief, responsible for screening visitors and ensuring that his master was safe and secure.

Abdullah, a former police officer, came to Peshawar in 1983 after being drawn to the Afghan jihad. He was among the first Arab volunteers who responded to the call for jihad when the Soviet Red Army invaded Afghanistan in December 1979 to save the crumbling Afghan communist regime. In fact, he reportedly joined the jihad before bin Laden, Sheikh Omar Abdul Rahman and the late Sheikh Abdullah Azzam, a Palestinian-Jordanian who gave up his job as a lecturer in Islamabad's Islamic University and was responsible for luring a large number of Arab nationals to receive military training and fight in Afghanistan. Abdullah was constantly at bin Laden's side, moving first to the Pakistani frontier city of Peshawar and then to Afghanistan. His death in a recent US bombing raid near Kabul was a big loss for bin Laden and Al Qaeda.

Despite his blindness, Sheikh Omar Abdul Rahman had also come to Peshawar on his way to Afghanistan to take part in the Afghan jihad. His two young sons, Mohammad and Abu Asem, found themselves stranded in Afghanistan after the retreat of the Soviet troops because they risked arrest on return to Egypt. They vowed revenge against the US while talking to me in Khost if their old, ailing father was not released. Abu Yasir Rifa'i Ahmad Taha, a leader of Sheikh Abdul Rahman's Al Jamaah Al Islamiah, was another prominent Egyptian staying in Afghanistan. So were Arab nationals from almost every West Asian and African country, who said they all came to fight the invading Red Army and seek the blessings of Allah by embracing martyrdom. Most of their comrades were able to return home, some picking up the gun in places like Algeria and Egypt to bring about an Islamic revolution. Many of those who could not go, about a thousand, were part of Al Qaeda. In fact, some of them wanted to focus on the struggles in their respective countries rather than becoming involved in violence elsewhere in the Arab world or against the US and its Western allies.

Islamists such as Al-Zawahiri and Abdullah were high on the US list of wanted men as well as bin Laden. During Operation Enduring Freedom, Washington was led to believe that the Saudi-born Islamist was holed up in one of his Tora Bora cave hideouts in the Spinghar (White Mountain) range. A US government official also said bin Laden had been heard giving orders to his fighters on a short-circuit radio. The relentless US bombing of Tora Bora, probably the heaviest in this century of a specific target in a battlefield, was thus hardly surprising.

The US was ready to pay any amount of money to its Afghan proxies and use tonnes of bombs to get bin Laden. It hired the services of the Northern and Eastern alliances and anti-Taliban Pashtun groups. What it achieved, however, was only the partial decimation of Al Qaeda. The battle began in the Tora Bora and Mailawa mountains before shifting to the Agam and Wazir valleys in the Spinghar. Throughout the campaign, anti-Taliban commanders kept saying that they would be able to secure the unconditional surrender of the Al Qaeda fighters. Yet, it was obvious that the three commanders were working at cross-purposes. All were anxious to impress the Americans and win their favour. But they were seldom able to provide sufficient number of fighters to organise swift ground offensives. Special US forces moved in larger numbers to Tora Bora to direct bombing missions and carry out operations once it became clear that the anti-Taliban commanders were not effective. However, there was no evidence that the American soldiers actively engaged the enemy. Instead, they kept their Afghan proxy fighters ahead of them to avoid casualties and intervened only to conduct search and mopping up operations.

In the end, a commander claimed 200 Al Qaeda fighters were captured and 80 killed in the Tora Bora campaign. Though the figures appeared impressive, it ought to be remembered that the Al Qaeda men were no match for US firepower and anti-Taliban manpower. That the Al Qaeda fighters were able to resist the onslaught for several days and at times escape despite claims that they were surrounded showed their fierce determination. Their defiance was further on evidence when about a dozen wounded Al Qaeda fighters admitted in a government hospital in Kandahar died fighting rather than becoming US prisoners of war.

The anti-Taliban commanders in Tora Bora also failed on another front: they could not win over the local people. The locals were clearly unhappy that the Afghans at the behest of the US were attacking the stateless Arabs and bin Laden's followers.

In comparison, the Al Qaeda fighters holed up in Tora Bora proved smart. They bought precious time by offering to surrender and seeking extensions in deadlines. It is possible they made use of this time to shift bin Laden and some of his top lieutenants to safer places. So, it was anti-climactic when anti-Taliban commander Hazrat Ali announced that bin Laden was untraceable even after having cleared Tora Bora of all Al Qaeda fighters.

Though the 31 Arabs who made it to Pakistan from Tora Bora were not lucky because they were caught in the tribal Kurram Agency, others may have found refuge in Afghan villages, fled to adjoining provinces in Afghanistan or sneaked through the long and porous Pakistan-Afghan border. Pakistan's tribal areas quickly became the focus of attention as one of bin Laden's likely destinations. It is certain though that he would never venture to enter Pakistan and risk being caught. The fate of some Taliban leaders who were captured by Pakistani authorities and handed over to the Americans would likely prompt him not to enter Pakistan. If still alive, he is most likely to be somewhere in Afghanistan even though the former Taliban interior minister Mulla Abdul Razzaq has said that bin Laden had left the country. There are many Afghans, among them his loyal cook, Tooti, who would be willing to offer any sacrifice to protect him. Having publicly expressed his wish to die as a martyr fighting the Americans, bin Laden will probably not run away from Afghanistan and abandon his loyal band.

Note that bin Laden has not toned down his rhetoric. By accusing the West of showing hatred towards Islam and by charging the US with supporting Israel to punish the Palestinians, bin Laden is attempting to reach out to the Muslim masses who feel let down by their pro-West rulers. He has referred to the West's crusades against Islam and the US bombing of Afghanistan to add punch to his argument. By referring to terrorism against the US as 'benign' or 'blessed' and as retaliation against those who kill Muslims, bin Laden has tried to justify his jihad against America and Israel. It is an intelligent argument aimed at winning the hearts and minds of Muslims worldwide.

His position has not changed since May 1998 when he first made public the fatwa issued by scores of Ulema declaring jihad against the US and Israel. He called his newly launched organisation the International Islamic Front for Jihad Against the US and Israel to emphasise the same point. He reiterated his call for jihad in accordance with the fatwa when I met him in December 1998 near Kandahar, south-western Afghanistan, for an interview. The fiat called upon the Muslims to carry on jihad to liberate Islamic holy sites, including the Ka'aba in Makkah and the Al-Aqsa mosque in Jerusalem. Most probably, he reasoned, the anti-US bombings took place because of the calls and warnings given by his Front. 'If the instigation for jihad against the Americans and Israelis to liberate the Al-Aqsa mosque and Holy Ka'aba is considered a crime,' he declared in that interview, 'let history be witness that I am a criminal.'

'I picked up a Kalashnikov and after feeling the weapon in my hands, found that it was ready to talk to the *mushrikeen* (enemy) . . . I felt ecstatic at the thought of enemy soldiers falling.'

Maulana Masood Azhar: Jaish-e-Mohammed

Harinder Baweja

India discovered him at 2 p.m. on 1 October 2001, soon after a Tata Sumo rammed the heavily guarded gate of the Jammu and Kashmir Assembly in Srinagar. The thirty-nine mangled bodies strewn around the Assembly compound bore the unmistakable stamp of pan-Islamic jihad. The perpetrator: Maulana Masood Azhar, chief of the Jaish-e-Mohammed or the Army of the Prophet.

As for the Maulana, he had begun to discover himself fairly early on. Soon after he had cleared his Class VIII exams, in fact, when Mufti Sayeed, a friend of his father's persuaded him to let the young Azhar join the Jamia Islamia at the Binori mosque in Karachi.

The Mufti was one of the teachers at the Jamia Islamia and it was no ordinary school for Azhar soon found himself in the company of students who were under the influence of leaders of the Harkat-ul-Mujahideen (HUM), a militant organisation that was then active in Afghanistan and later extended its activities to Kashmir. The HUM leaders – it was no coincidence – had also been students at the same madrasa in the Binori mosque complex.

Azhar passed the *almia* (Islamic) examination with distinction in 1989 when he was 21. At an age when most youth are plotting their professional future, Azhar had already made up his mind on what he would do. He had been deeply influenced by the HUM leaders and by his fellow students who were not just Pakistanis but Arab, Sudanese and Bangladeshi nationals. Some of them had already departed for neighbouring Afghanistan and soon after he met Maulana Fazlur Rahman Khalil, the HUM chief, Azhar too was on his way for what he called *tarbiat* or training.

Sent to Yuvar, a training camp in Afghanistan, Azhar soon found that while he'd topped the *almia* in Karachi, he was having great difficulty when it came to obstacle races and weapons. The stodgy 5 ft 3" figure could not complete the mandatory 40-day training programme. He admitted later to his interrogators in Srinagar, where he was arrested in 1994, that this was 'because of his poor physique'.

He returned to the Jamia Islamia from Afghanistan and took up a job as a teacher and his 'literary skills' – knowledge of Islam and jihad – soon saw him bringing out a magazine called *Sada-i-Mujahid* or *Knock of the Mujahideen*. It carried articles on HUM's activities and the war in Afghanistan and free copies of it were distributed after Friday prayers and at functions held by the Harkat. This was in 1989 and a year later, the Harkat had opened offices in various cities across Pakistan, including Hyderabad, Gujranwala, Lahore and Islamabad. A recruitment drive was also launched and the qualifications were simple: only those with beards and only those who had been trained in Afghanistan.

Khalil, the HUM chief, found that Azhar was not only qualified to bring out the magazine but also that he was a skilled orator and so started a department of motivation under the Maulana's tutelage. It were these skills that were to play a lethal role in the insurgency that first started as an indigenous movement in Kashmir in 1989.

The Maulana may never have turned his attention to India or Kashmir – a family member revealed – were it not for the demolition of the Babri Masjid at Ayodhya on 6 December 1992. Till then, he was happy playing the role of a 'journalist' through *Sada-i-Mujahid*. What the Maulana was doing was spreading the message of jihad and collecting funds for his comrades in Afghanistan. Impressed with his skilled oratory and his ability to procure donations through his speeches, Khalil encouraged the Maulana to undertake foreign tours for this purpose.

Azhar, who first obtained his passport under his own name, was soon on his way to Saudi Arabia on a Haj pilgrimage and managed to collect Rs 300,000 in a matter of a few days. He extolled the virtues of jihad and the role of the HUM in other countries too and soon found himself in Zambia where he stayed for a month, occupying himself with giving speeches in mosques. By the end of his trip, Azhar had again collected Rs 2.2 million in the name of religious education. Similarly, a trip to Birmingham, Nottingham, Leicester and London in the UK saw him expand his network of contacts and his financial kitty.

The first point of conflict with the Pakistani establishment – which till then was quite comfortable with the role of the HUM in Afghanistan – came after the Soviet withdrawal. Due to the international pressure being mounted on Pakistan to rein in the jihadis, the establishment was forced to make a few arrests. The approximately 500 arrested militants were then pressurised to leave Pakistani soil for the UAE but the fear of persecution saw them make their way to Somalia via Sudan where they joined the ranks of the Ittehad-e-Islami.

The militants kept in touch with the HUM and wrote back to say that the Pakistani army, deployed in aid of the United Nations, was working against the interests of Islam by targetting the Ittehad-e-Islami cadre. This is when the confrontation between Khalil and the Pakistani establishment first started. The HUM chief asked Azhar to contact senior Pakistani journalists and persuade them to send a team of reporters to Kenya where top leaders of the Ittehad group were staying. Azhar managed to do that and with his chief, Khalil, accompanied the team to Nairobi. They returned to Pakistan a week later to write lengthy articles in various journals which, they were happy to find, embarrassed the government.

Azhar was now asked to go to 'Azad Kashmir' to meet Sajjad Afghani. Sajjad was a sharpshooter who had performed bravely against the Russians and Azhar had first met him at the training camp in Yuvar. The timing of this meeting was important: he had been called in January 1993, a month after the Babri Masjid demolition. The purpose: to aid the Kashmiri mujahideen in their struggle against 'Hindu India'. While in Muzaffarabad, Azhar met Maulana Farooq Kashmiri, the chief of operations for 'Indian-held Kashmir', and together they toured various places in 'Azad Kashmir' addressing public meetings in which they spoke of the need to 'liberate' Kashmir from Indian occupation. On the same tour, Sajjad Afghani was asked to take over the command of all military operations in Kashmir. He was to get there by first going to Bangladesh since the passes along the Line of Control were covered with high walls of snow. Dhaka, the Bangladeshi capital, was chosen for another reason. Maulvi Kalimullah, a schoolmate of Azhar's at the Binori mosque, was now running a madrasa in Dhaka and would be there to help Sajjad cross the border into India. Azhar flew to Dhaka with Sajjad and returned to Karachi while Sajjad was launched into India to give the Kashmiri mujahideen a fighting edge.

A year later it was Azhar's turn to go to Kashmir to further boost the morale of the 'freedom fighters'. Azhar flew to Dhaka and then to Delhi, this time on a Portuguese passport. The person who landed in Delhi's Indira Gandhi International airport in the early hours of the morning of 29 January 1994 had changed his name from Maulana Masood Azhar to Adam Issa. The immigration officer who inspected Azhar alias Issa's passport commented that he didn't look Portuguese but quickly stamped the passport when told that he was of Gujarati origin.

Azhar hailed a taxi, not to some remote guesthouse, but to the government-owned Ashoka Hotel, where he checked in for the night. His life was too precious to risk an arrest, so Azhar had been instructed to stay at an expensive hotel. He had also been asked to call a carpet dealer. The next morning he had two visitors knocking on his door: the carpet dealer and the chief of operations of the Jammu region. But it was not Srinagar that he wanted to head for. He had another destination in mind. And so it was Lucknow that he went to and from there to Ayodhya.

His visit to the disputed site where all that was left of the Babri Masjid was rubble is an experience best narrated in the Maulana's own words: 'I remember the day I was standing there. In front of me lay the Babri Masjid in ruins. Angrily, I was stamping the ground, squashing the Indian soil with my shoes and saying, "O Babri Masjid, we are ashamed, O Babri Masjid, we are sorry . . . you were a sign of our glorious past and we will not rest till we restore you to your former glory."' These lines, in fact, became part of all his speeches, words that helped indoctrinate and motivate the Harkat cadre. But before he could reach Srinagar and start doing that, Azhar visited various Muslim localities in India where his speeches were recorded and cassettes distributed.

Azhar had come a long way indeed. Born in Bahawalpur on 10 July 1968, where he lived for the first ten years with six sisters and four brothers, Azhar was just another child, being brought up in a lower middle class home. Allah Bakhsh Shabir, his father, taught at a local school and was a small-time entrepreneur who ran a small dairy and poultry farm. He was also an extremely religious man and heads of various madrasas were an inner part of his contact circle. Mufti Sayeed, the teacher at the Jamia Islamia at Karachi's Binori mosque, was one such friend and this is how Azhar made his way from Bahawalpur in Punjab to the madrasa in Karachi.

Religious indoctrination from a young age and the fact that Khalil, the Harkat chief, spotted him at Binori – from where the organisation was recruiting cadres for Pakistan – ensured Azhar's entry into the battlefield of jihad. Being a trusted aide of Khalil, it was only a matter of time before Azhar embarked on a journey to Srinagar to motivate the Kashmiri 'freedom fighters'. He looked forward to the trip for another reason: he would be meeting Sajjad Afghani with whom he had developed a close bond. So, from Ayodhya, Azhar came back to Delhi and took a flight to Srinagar. Escorted straight from the airport to a mosque in the city's downtown area, Azhar was asked to wait for Sajjad Afghani who would come as soon as it was possible for him to evade the security dragnet and find his way there safely.

Sajjad and Azhar were too precious for the cause and had been directed not to unduly take any risks. Besides, Azhar had come there for an important mission. Apart from motivating the cadre, he also had to ensure that the mujahideen belonging to the two separate groups of Harkat-ul-Jehad-e-Islami and the Harkat-ul-Mujhaideen merge under the new name of Harkat-ul-Ansar and work under one umbrella. These instructions had been relayed some months ago but back in Pakistan, Khalil had not received any confirmation of the merger. Few dared disobey Azhar. He had by then become respected as a great Islamic ideologue who had travelled through 25 different countries with the sole aim of propagating jihad and collecting funds for this 'holy' mission.

Word had already reached Srinagar and the neighbouring

district of Anantnag that the Maulana had arrived and that he would soon be visiting them and addressing them on their cause. Sajjad joined him at the mosque in Lal Bazaar that evening and both of them set off for a remote village in Anantnag, about 70 km from Srinagar. The meeting or *majlis-e-jehad* that took place here is best described in Azhar's own words: 'About 25 armed mujahideen were gathered at a small house in the village. They greeted us warmly and soon a religious discourse began. The young men's chests were decorated with magazines and within them burned the flame of courage and bravery. All of them were listening to me intently and their AK-47s lay cradled in their laps like children in their mother's care. Some of them also had carbines and rocket launchers that they must have seized from the Army. Three or four of our soldiers were guarding the door downstairs and they had wanted to join us too but then duty came first and they had to contend with listening to me over their wireless sets. After the *majlis* ended, my brothers stretched out on the floor and I decided to go down and join the mujahideen who were on guard duty. Before I did that, I picked up a Kalashnikov and after feeling the weapon in my hands, found that it was ready to talk to the *mushrikeen* (enemy). The bullet was in the chamber and it was ready to fire and I felt ecstatic at the thought of enemy soldiers falling . . . my joy knew no bounds as I held the loaded gun in my hands.'

Azhar spent two days in the Valley speaking to the mujahideen and was looking forward to the following day which was a Friday because Sajjad wanted him to deliver prayers at the Jama Masjid. Azhar's joy at the prospect of meeting his fellow brothers was, however, short lived for that Friday – 10 February 1994 – Sajjad and he were arrested after their car broke down on the way to the mosque and they were trying to hail an auto rickshaw.

Their arrests came as a big blow to Khalil and the Pakistan establishment that had embarked on the new strategy of pushing foreign mercenaries into Kashmir to give the militants a cutting edge. The Indian Army had nabbed the two most important people who were supposed to inject jihadi fervour into an insurgency, which had initially started as a battle for 'independence'.

It was soon after his arrest that this writer met Azhar. His behaviour in custody then, in February 1994, was no different from the kind of treatment meted out to me in Kabul by the Taliban in October 1996. Azhar refused to look me in the eye for religion forbade eye contact with women. It didn't matter at all that the Indian Army surrounded him or that he was in captivity. He had no problems, rather, no reservations narrating what he had done in the two days that he had spent in the Valley. He was fortunate, I remember him telling me, that Allah had chosen him for what he called an Islamic duty and his only regret was that he had been captured and not killed. Had he been tortured, I asked him. Driven by rage – he broke his own rule – and looking me straight in the eye said sarcastically, 'No, the Army has been showering me with petals.'

He spent months after that in the hands of various interrogating officials drawn from different agencies like the Intelligence Bureau and the Research and Analysis Wing. The interrogating officer for Kashmir's counter intelligence wing, after several days trying to break Azhar, interestingly noted in his report that 'he (Azhar) was not himself involved in any subversive activity in Kashmir.'

Unknown to his interrogators, the Pakistan establishment was devising desperate strategies to secure the Maulana's release. The first plan of action was put into place within a few months of his arrest. In June, the same year – 1994 – the Harkat-ul-Ansar kidnapped two British nationals while they were trekking near Pahalgam in Kashmir's Anantnag district. One of them, Kim Housego, was the son of David Housego, a well-known Delhi-based journalist. High on the list of demands put forth by the HUA was the release of Azhar. But when that didn't work, another plot was hatched four months later in the month of October.

This time, Omar Sheikh (now implicated in the kidnapping and death of Daniel Pearl, *Wall Street Journal's* South Asia correspondent) was sent to India with the express purpose of kidnapping foreigners to secure the Maulana's release. He managed to befriend an American and three British tourists and keep them chained at a safe house on the outskirts of Delhi but was soon nabbed by the police. Like Azhar, he found himself in jail and both languished there for years without much progress on their legal cases.

Pakistan did not give up despite Sheikh's arrest and the next year, in 1995, five more foreigners were kidnapped by the Al Faran, a front name for the HUA. Again, the name that topped the list of the militants the Al Faran wanted released in exchange for the hostages was Azhar's. Kashmir authorities continued negotiations with the captors for many months before the link snapped and the hostages were given up for dead. The Maulana's importance for the Pakistani establishment can be judged from the fact that their High Commission in India approached the Ministry for External Affairs for his release on the plea that he was a journalist.

Technically, that is how the Maulana began – as the editor of *Sada-i-Mujahid* – but he was much more than that. As master motivator, his mind was more lethal than an AK-47, his words more dangerous than bullets. His speeches hit home and indoctrinated many minds. Even when in jail, Azhar continued with his writing, smuggling letters out with help from sympathetic jail sources.

Azhar was finally freed in exchange for passengers aboard IC-814 – hijacked from Kathmandu to Kandahar in the last week of December 1999. The desperate attempt to secure his release – after several rounds of kidnappings didn't do the trick – was mounted after the prison riot in the Jammu jail in June 1999. The riot started after a daring escape bid by the foreign mercenaries and local militants. Sajjad Afghani and other inmates had been secretly digging a tunnel through the jail and had managed to do so without being detected. Azhar too had checked out the tunnel but wriggled out after going in six feet saying it needed to be broadened if big-built people like him were to get through.

The escape bid failed and Sajjad was killed in the firing. Sajjad's killing, in fact, pressed alarm buttons in Pakistan and the authorities feared that Azhar too would be similarly killed. Always wiser only on hindsight, Indian authorities now believe that the hijacking was staged to ensure Azhar's flight to safety.

The negotiating team – drawn from the Ministry of External Affairs and the intelligence agencies – gave up only after they realised that the hijackers would not stop short of blowing up the plane. The only thing the hijackers did do was scale down their demands: at one point they were even demanding that Sajjad Afghani's body be dug up and handed back to them. What they were not willing to settle for was getting back other militants in lieu of either Azhar or Omar Sheikh.

The 'journalist' in Azhar helped him develop sources and keep abreast of developments, not only during the hijacking but also all through his years in jail. After Sajjad's death, Azhar went into an introspective phase and his mood changed only after he managed to convince a lawyer – who visited the Jammu jail – to get him a photograph of Sajjad's grave. He even managed to smuggle out a long letter he wrote to Sajjad's parents, the contents of which provide a rare insight into Azhar's psychology: 'Honourable parents, man sometimes pins his hopes on small trifling things and then waits for them to come true . . . but Allah Ta'ala, the magnanimous one, instead of granting him trifles, gives him far greater. It was my cherished hope that I would come to your house and give you the glad tidings that your son had been set free. I used to dream that I would attend his wedding and as the priest, deliver his marriage sermon . . . instead of freedom and marriage, Allah decided to give you exceptional honour and unparalleled happiness. He accepted your son in his divine mercy and took Sajjad out of prison and made him a guest of His own. Instead of marrying him to some mortal woman, Allah married him to the Hoors of Jannah. I congratulate you for this honour, for the blessing that you have received . . . everyone has to taste the flavour of death but the death your son has tasted is delicious and sweet. A death that is a million times better than life, which life itself envies; a death, which Allah says, must not be called death . . . .

' . . . Respected parents, Islam has fallen upon such distressing times. The infidels are trying to efface Islam and the Muslims from the face of the earth. The irony is that the Muslims themselves, out of greed for this world, have pushed Islam out of their homes. In such conditions, whoever stands up and fights for Islam, gives up his very life for its supremacy. How dear he must be to Allah. You should be felicitated that your son is among those dear to Allah. In these distressing times, when Muslims have lost their identity, your son by embracing martyrdom has focused the world's attention upon this unique characteristic of Islam. Millions of Allah's blessings are upon him who even in prison could never be subjugated. Not for a single moment did he bow to his captors. They beat him and tortured him till they got tired but he untiringly proclaimed the supremacy of Islam. Annoyed beyond measure by his challenging cry, the enemy often told him that he would die in jail because of his religious notions. Sajjad used to scoff at them and tell them that he wanted nothing else and that he had left home in search of martyrdom. At such times, his eyes shone with intensity and fervour.

'The other time I saw him so happy was the day he left us on his final journey. There was a deep, peaceful smile upon his face that I shall never forget for as long as I live. As he had been brutally tortured and his death had been so sudden, I was crying continuously till I saw his face and my spirits lifted in joy and in gratitude to Allah. Your son preferred courage to cowardice, piety to sinfulness. The reward of a single day spent on jihad is better than this world and everything in it. You need not be ashamed or sad because he was not in prison for any crime but for having tried to safeguard the honour of his Kashmiri mothers and sisters and for having fought for the greatness of Islam . . . I want to write so much more but you must be aware of the restrictions on us prisoners. It needs the help of Allah Ta'ala for a letter to be sent from here. This year, in the month of Ramadan, all of us had earnestly prayed for martyrdom or for release from jail. Sajjad's prayers have been granted while the rest of us are waiting. Who will be the one to lie next to Sajjad in the Jammu graveyard, no one knows. If I become the lucky one then I ask you to pray for me too . . . '

According to Jammu jail authorities, Azhar too spent much time in prayer and would interact, if at all, only with other foreign militants lodged in the same prison. Nursing nothing but sheer contempt for the non-Muslim officials, he had little fear of reprisal for he would call them infidels to their faces. In custody, he also exhibited leadership qualities and sorted out differences that would often crop up between Pakistani mercenaries and Kashmiri militants. It was against the principle of Islam, he would tell them, and urge them to stay united because their cause was the same.

Booked under the Terrorist and Disruptive Activities Act (TADA), the case against him progressed slowly. Subsequently, he was also charged with the jailbreak attempt. At a loss about what to do with foreign militants – as opposed to today when the unwritten orders are to kill – Azhar spent close to six years in jail but it was only after his release that the Indian authorities realised that he was a live bomb that had been ticking for all the six years that he was behind bars.

Scared that the hijackers would use their own bombs to blow up the hijacked plane and its passengers, a shamefaced Jaswant Singh, Minister for External Affairs, flew him, Omar Sheikh and a third militant, Mushtaq Zargar, in his own plane and landed in Kandahar to secure the hostages on board the hijacked Indian Airlines plane. It was clear to most that this could only be an invitation to terror. For Azhar himself, it was a moment when he had been blessed. His flight to freedom is, once again, best described in his own words. 'The plane was flying high and heading for Pakistan and soon it would be over Baluchistan and then over Afghanistan. I turned to look back and caught the curiosity-filled glance of Mushtaq Zargar, Kashmir's notable commander. Another mujahideen companion, Omar Sheikh, was sitting a few rows ahead of me. Each of us had three guards around us. I counted the others and they totalled around 90. Jaswant Singh, the Minister of Bharat, sat in the very first row. He had a personal physician with him who gave him some tablets. The cabin crew politely offered us refreshments but we declined saying we were fasting. We were neither hungry nor thirsty but lusting for the freedom that would soon be ours. The historic moment arrived when the plane started descending . . .

' . . . The runway flashed by and I was a mixture of emotions. The land where the plane had touched down, everything belonging to it, was intensely dear to me. Mullah Omar, the person whose deep love filled my heart, lived here in Kandahar. He, whose presence is a true blessing for the Muslims, had made

Islam proud. When I was in prison, I desperately yearned to behold this city and kiss the hand of Mullah Omar . . . the plane was racing towards the airport building and the sight of the beautiful faces of the thousands of Taliban armed guards was adding joy to my heart. I was surprised to see such a vast number of guards lining the runway . . . I thought it would take hours for the formalities to be completed and an unknown fear gnawed at me. I felt like breaking the door of the plane and running like a mad man down the tarmac. As soon as the door opened, a member of the Indian team came towards me and said "Maulana sahab, come with me quickly". I told him to wait so I could tie my turban, since this was the land of the Taliban. As soon as my feet touched the ground, my heart was transformed . . .

' . . . Taliban officials greeted us at the foot of the stairs. Maulvi Muhammad Akhtar Usmani, the Kandahar Corps Commander, was among them and after a warm embrace he showed me into a car. A few feet away stood the Indian plane that had been hijacked a week ago. Our car came to a halt. The Corps Commander walked to the plane and said something to the hijackers above. As I watched mesmerised, two masked men came down with the use of a rope ladder and ran towards our car and hugged me in a warm embrace. A storm of emotions washed over us and tears welled in our eyes. Had the world seen those tears, they would have known why these softhearted men – being called terrorists and extremists – had taken this step. It was because of the atrocities committed by India and its barbaric treatment that had driven these men [sic]. I couldn't help thinking of one thing: the day my hands had been tied behind my back and I had been pushed into a truck was a Friday. The truck had headed for the prison where my life in captivity had started and today was a Friday too. Both my hands were free and I was sitting in a Taliban car heading towards freedom, a freedom about which my prayer is: Ya Allah make it a precursor to the liberation of Kashmir, the Babri Masjid and the Masjid-Al-Aqsa (Jerusalem).'

Azhar's entry into Afghanistan was as dramatic as his exit from India. Not only was he personally flown by Jaswant Singh, he had also been escorted to Delhi from Jammu by A.S. Dulat, the RAW chief who is now an adviser in the Prime Minister's

Office. What the Government of India obviously didn't realise then was that they were freeing a deadly trio.

The association between Azhar and Omar Sheikh did not start with the rescue plan, but in 1993 when Omar came to Pakistan from London where he was studying at the London School of Economics (LSE). Born and brought up in England, Omar had an aggressive nature even as a child and often picked fights in school for being referred to as a 'Paki'. He was twice suspended from school for objecting to 'racial remarks' but remained a bright student, picking up a scholarship of 6,000 pounds for getting good grades. But what went passionately with school books was his penchant for Islamic literature and his consciousness of being a Muslim.

While at the LSE – after he failed to get admission either at Stanford or Harvard – Omar joined the Islamic Society, while also pursuing an interest in arm-wrestling. Not only did he participate in the world-level, arm-wrestling championship in Geneva in October 1992, but also made it to the fifth position at London's arm-wrestling meet. It was the activities of the Islamic Society that made a mark on him and interestingly, he had with him – in class and in the Society – a friend in Hussain Nawaz Sharif, son of former Pakistan Prime Minister Nawaz Sharif. Hussain contested the elections for the post of the Society's general secretary but lost.

In November 1992, the Society decided to observe 'Bosnia week' and collected funds for the Bosnian cause by showing films on atrocities against Muslims. Images of starving children and crimes against pregnant women played an important role in shaping his mind. As he told his interrogators in India after his arrest, 'Hussain Nawaz Sharif and I decided to do something for the cause but no one got down to actually doing anything concrete.'

Omar, however, decided that it wasn't enough to just collect funds. Enquiries about Bosnia soon saw him join the Muslim Aid and Islamic Relief Agency of which famous pop singer Cat Stevens was the president. Unhappy with mere relief work, Omar – on a subsequent trip to Pakistan – made contact with HUM chief Fazlur Rehman Khalil and soon found himself at a

training camp where he first came into contact with Azhar –
not with the person but his voice. Omar found himself totally
taken in with the Maulana's speech, reverberating through the
training camp. 'The true road to Islam is the Afghan way . . . I
don't want to see the youth wasting their time in cricket or
football. I am interested in those who are willing to wield the
AK-47, pistols and rocket launchers.'

Unknown to Omar, Azhar had already met his father on a
trip to London. Omar and Azhar finally came face to face in
December 1993 when the Maulana convinced the London-bred
youth to concentrate on Kashmir instead of Bosnia as there were
already enough fighters for that struggle. India, he said, had to
be taught a lesson and Kashmir was to be liberated. Few came
into contact with Azhar without being mesmerised and Omar
was no exception.

The day they set foot in Kandahar, the two apparently called
on Mullah Omar and Osama bin Laden who they thought were
the biggest champions of Islam. Even after they reached Pakistan,
a week later, the two kept in constant touch and Azhar soon
came to the forefront on 31 January 2000 – exactly a month
after the touchdown in Kandahar – and announced the formation
of the Jaish-e-Mohammed. Addressing a gathering of about
10,000 armed followers outside a mosque in Karachi, Azhar
thundered, 'I have come here because it is my duty to tell you
that Muslims should not rest in peace until we have destroyed
America and India. Kashmir has to be liberated from Indian rule.
Soldiers of Islam have come from twelve countries to free Kashmir.
Our organisation has nothing to do with politics. We fight for
religion and do not believe in the concept of nations. We want
Islam to rule the world.' Charged by his fiery speech, the crowd
responded with slogans of 'Death to India, death to the United
States.'

Unlike his friend Sajjad Afghani who had been married to
the Hoors of Jannah, Azhar decided to marry a mortal but
decided on his wedding day to undertake a six-month journey
and stay away from his wife. What he was doing for six months
was motivating and training the Jaish cadre – most of them
dedicated HUM fighters who switched sides. Six years in jail had,

in fact, made no difference to Azhar's jihad factory. If at all, it had only expanded.

Azhar had wasted no time in launching the Jaish-e-Mohammed for he now had two vital men – Omar and Mushtaq Zargar – by his side. Omar like him was a die-hard jihadi and Zargar had a network of contacts in the Kashmir Valley, particularly in Srinagar, from where he had started his journey as a militant and had come to head the Al Umar, a dreaded insurgency group. While Azhar was the motivator and fund collector, Zargar helped him recruit local Kashmiris for the Jaish. Omar was the arms instructor, trained as he was in the use of small and heavy weapons. Together, their motto was: jihad is worship and obedience to Allah, and that Jaish was the need of the hour to revive the spirit of the holy war.

While its main office was in Islamabad, the Jaish started a training camp at Balakot in the North West Frontier Province to train these holy warriors. Initially, only a couple of tents, the training camp soon became a huge complex comprising several buildings which included a residential complex, a kitchen, guest houses, a dispensary and a mosque. Encouraged by the ISI to wage its war against India, the training camp operates quite openly: it does not have a boundary wall but about 400 armed compatriots are deployed at vantage points around the perimeter where youth are trained in batches of 800 to 1000. While there are training camps in other Pakistani provinces, the one at Balakot is the most elaborate and is reputedly run by Yousuf, a Christian convert from Sindh who is married to Azhar's sister.

Outside the perimeter of the training camps, Zargar and Azhar were also influencing minds in the Kashmir Valley and with the help of maulvis in mosques, training them to become suicide bombers. It was the Jaish, in fact, which introduced and spread this new terror tool to devastating effect. Security officials in Srinagar were surprised to find in April 2000 that a local, 17-year-old boy had decided to convert his body into a guided missile. Also shocked were his parents who only knew their son as a shy, introvert who usually spent his time studying so he could go on and fulfil his dream of becoming a doctor. Afaq even got himself photographed wearing a doctor's coat and a stethoscope and kept the framed picture in his room.

The youngest of three brothers, none in the family thought Afaq's behaviour had changed when he started spending nights in the local mosque next door. It was good, his parents thought, that he was taking an interest in religion. They were not overly worried even when, on some evenings at home, Afaq would read the Quran by candlelight. It soon became a routine – the flickering flame and the Quran and then Afaq would start reading out aloud and start crying.

Till one day – when he just left home never to return. He had driven a stolen red Maruti car laden with explosives to the high security barrier bordering the 15 Corps Army Headquarters in Srinagar and blown himself up. The explosion heralded the advent of the suicide bomber, with live bombs that caused heavy destruction of men and material with no real cost to the militant group itself.

Flush with funds and men, willing to die, the Army of Mohammed is one of the most potent groups operating in Kashmir and has, according to Indian intelligence agencies, 'carried out more than 100 attacks on security forces and their strategic installations.' The most lethal attack came on 1 October 2001 – three weeks after the World Trade Center towers collapsed in New York – and Azhar was quick to claim credit. He withdrew it the next day, purportedly under pressure from his mentors in the Pakistani establishment. But that his handlers could hold sway over him was evident even in March 2000 when Azhar was put under house arrest during the visit of President Bill Clinton.

Under pressure from the United States – after the attack on the Indian Parliament on 13 December 2001 – Pakistan President General Pervez Musharraf was forced to freeze the accounts of the Jaish, among other groups, and arrest the Maulana. But like Omar Sheikh – who is allowed to make phone calls to his father while in custody – Azhar too is allowed visitors.

Despite the ban on the Jaish, the organisation's activities though constrained have not come to a halt. Its office has shifted from Islamabad to Bahawalpur – Azhar's hometown – as Daniel Pearl found, much to his peril.

His kidnapping and killing only proved that despite the crackdown on the jihadi elements, there are enough who are still on the move; mujahideen who will not hesitate to propagate their own cause. Azhar may be in custody at the moment but his mindset will not change. It did not, even in the six years that he spent in Indian jails. Jihad is in his mind and it is that concept that he is wedded to. The suicide attack on the Srinagar assembly on 1 October shows that Azhar revisited India, if only, in spirit. But he had begun to discover himself much earlier. The young student who joined the madrasa at Karachi's Binori mosque is today the chief of the Jaish-e-Mohammad. Most wanted, not only for the weapon he wields, but for his mind.

'God has ordained every Muslim to fight until His rule is established. We have no option but to follow God's order.'

Hafiz Mohammed Saeed: Lashkar-e-Toiba

Amir Mir

At first sight – he is an academician – a jovial man who wears an easy smile on his face and, invariably, a Turkish cap on his head . . . a *shalwar kameez*-clad man, thoroughly Eastern in dress and habit, who is friendly and humble towards those who listen carefully to him . . . probably a person whose only introduction to cosmetics has been the henna that is regularly applied to his long beard – a regular feature on a regular face in this part of the world.

At first sight – it is a face that hardly begs for the camera. Look closer – it is a face that shies away from cameras as a rule. It has good reason to: Islam, the much un-photographed man says, forbids the capture of human images. Human lives, however, are another matter. For Professor Hafiz Mohammed Saeed, killing is a pious man's obligation: it is his duty 'to destroy the forces of evil and disbelief'. And the Professor is a very pious man.

His kind of piety has also given him dubious distinctions. An uncrowned terror king till the suicide attack on the Indian Parliament House in New Delhi on 13 December 2001, Saeed headed the Lashkar-e-Toiba, the militant arm of the innocently titled Markaz Dawa Wal Irshad (the Centre for Religious Learning and Propagation). Dreaded for its guerrilla attacks in Kashmir and well known for the infamous attack on the Red Fort in New Delhi on 22 December 2000, the Lashkar is the Professor's brainchild, crafted through an interpretation of militant Islam. Statistics also bear out that the Lashkar-e-Toiba is no less pious than its ameer and founder. The website of the Markaz Irshad, in fact, proudly displays the cold equations of terror:

> ▶ 'During the last eleven years of jihad in Kashmir, 14,369 Indian soldiers were killed as against 1,016 Lashkar-e-Toiba militants.

> In 1999, eleven *fidayeen* (suicide) missions in Kashmir (that is, what Pakistan refers to as Held Kashmir) killed 258 Indian soldiers and officers.

> In 2000, by the grace of Allah, the mujahideen successfully carried out 98 *fidayeen* missions in which 891 Indian soldiers including three colonels, 10 majors, one commandant, one captain, three engineers and a number of JCOs were killed.'

At Muridke, 45 km from Lahore, which the bulky and bearded Professor Saeed used as his base – till Washington banned the Lashkar and Pakistan followed suit by freezing its assets – there is no trace of the blood behind the figures. Just the impression, which the Professor likes to give, of a scholarly man. But he is much more than that. Outwardly a simple Punjabi, who speaks in the tongue of the region, he has broken a fifty-three-year-old tradition: before him, the Pashtuns always led the jihad against India. Now, the Lashkar's ranks have just a few Pashtuns and even fewer Kashmiris.

Though the Lashkar-e-Toiba leader cultivates simplicity, he always moves under tight security. His preferred vehicle is the hardy Pajero. The Professor is generally surrounded by young followers with whom he is quite frank. The leader and his keen young group talk freely. Most of the youngsters are from big families that count close to ten members. The Professor favours the big-family norm, reasoning that greater Muslim numbers translate into many more fighters for jihad against the infidels. Once in the Lashkar, the youngsters are drawn into a pattern of community life, epitomised by the shared, common meal. All young men eat together using their fingers to pick food from a big, shared bowl or *parat*. This simple occasion is almost a rite, symbolising and encouraging fraternity among the comrades-in-arms.

The Professor himself comes from a close-knit family. He is married to the daughter of his maternal uncle, Hafiz Mohammad Abdullah Bahawalpuri, a well-known religious leader and renowned Ahle Hadith scholar. But, interestingly, he heads a very small family unit: one son and one daughter. Three members from among his widely dispersed family have been drawn into the organisation's ranks. His only son, the thirty-one-year-old

Talha, looks after the affairs of the Lashkar at its base camp in Muzaffarabad. His brother-in-law, Abdul Rehman Makki, is his close partner and holds an important position in the Markaz at Muridke. Makki spent many years in Saudi Arabia before settling down in Pakistan. The Professor's son-in-law Khalid Waleed is also associated with the Lashkar's organisational set-up in Lahore.

Two of the Professor's brothers live in the United States. One runs an Islamic centre while the other is pursuing his Ph.D studies in an American university. Both remain in constant touch with him. However, the Professor has never travelled to the United States or set foot anywhere in the West. And unlike most fundamentalists, he does not express deep hatred for it.

But the Professor's past has been bloody, with a cause for revenge. Thirty-six members of his family were murdered during Partition in 1947 when his father, Kamaluddin, an ordinary landlord, moved to Pakistan. Kamaluddin first tried to settle his family in the Sargodha district of Punjab, but finally chose Village 126 Janubi, in the Mianwali district. A government land grant to the settlers and hard work soon brought prosperity to the family, an effect that the Professor credits to Allah's bounty.

The Professor's parents were religious-minded and his mother used to teach the Holy Quran to her seven children, five of whom are still alive. The Professor was a good learner, and memorised the Quran. His favourite verse is: *Wajahidu Fee Sabilallah*: Wage a holy war in the name of God Almighty.

In college, the Professor furthered his religious interests. After graduating from the Government College at Sargodha, he went to Saudi Arabia for a Masters in Islamic Studies and in Arabic Lexicon from King Saud University, Riyadh. He frequently met religious scholars and even received special religious instruction. Indeed, his first job in Pakistan was as a research officer for the Islamic Ideological Council.

His current job could not have been more different. At fifty-five, he has just retired as professor of Islamic Studies from the University of Engineering and Technology in Lahore, and is fully devoted to his organisation. The fruits of that devotion are significant: in ten years, the Lashkar-e-Toiba, launched in 1991, has reportedly set up six private military training camps in Pakistan and in what is termed Azad Kashmir; has 2,500 offices across the country; and over two dozen launching camps along the Line of Control (LoC).

The Lashkar's jihadi network is the largest, the most efficient, and also has greater independence than other militant organisations since the Markaz Dawa Wal Irshad has a Wahabi orientation and does not have to follow any of the four Muslim religious leaders or imams. On the other hand, three other fundamentalist organisations – the Harkat-ul-Mujahideen, the Hizb-ul-Mujahideen, and the Jaish-e-Mohammed – are Deobandis and follow the imams.

The Lashkar – in an attempt to prove that the Kashmir insurgency is a freedom struggle – has announced that it is shifting its base to 'Indian-Held Kashmir' but it is Muridke that is the base of the Markaz Dawa Wal Irshad and the hub of the jihad machine. Spread over 200 acres, the complex houses teaching and residential facilities, complete with its own farms, mosques, fish-breeding ponds and stables.

Over 2,000 students are presently enrolled at the Centre and the teachers insist that all are Pakistanis. The education – Islamic and Western – is from the primary to the university level for both men and women. Students are doctrinated towards propagating Islam. The Markaz also has a modern-looking, computerised religious university, which has five related institutions. At least two dozen thoroughbred horses are used for training the Centre's students between the ages of eight to twenty years. These students, dressed in military uniforms, are imparted compulsory training in shooting and swimming. In fact, they are not allowed to cross the barbed periphery wire until they are 'mature'.

Photography of all living things which is anathema to the Professor is strictly prohibited. The Markaz Dawa Wal Irshad describes photo cameras, TV sets and films as un-Islamic and its students carry out periodic campaigns for the public destruction of cameras and TVs. Visitors are frisked for cigarettes and any other addictive substances, which are banned in the complex. The Muridke complex is also not just restricted to the Markaz Dawa Wal Irshad. Around the seminary, the organisation has bought land for supporters, who have built houses, shops and more mosques and centres of Islamic learning. 'We want like-minded people to get together,' says a resident.

Evidently that is happening. The organisation has transformed the land between Lahore and Gujranwala into an Islamic state that has banned music, television and smoking on its heavily guarded premises. Not even passing vehicles are allowed to play music which, the Professor believes, is strictly forbidden in Islam. The complex also has a garment factory, an iron foundry, a woodworks factory, a swimming pool and three residential colonies.

So far, Rs 30 million have been spent on the Markaz projects. Where has the money come from? Osama bin Laden, whisper rumours. It is alleged that the Saudi billionaire, a figure who has grown from being demonised by the West to being mythologised, rolled out a thick wad – Rs 10 million – for the construction of the Markaz's mosque. Osama bin Laden is even said to have financed Professor Saeed, his low-key, comrade-in-arms Zafar Iqbal, and a short-lived founder, Abdullah Azam, to launch the Markaz Dawa Wal Irshad in 1989.

Abdullah Azam was killed in a powerful bomb explosion at Peshawar, the capital of Pakistan's Frontier province, that very year. Zafar Iqbal, who used to head the Islamic Learning Centre at the government-run University of Engineering and Technology, Lahore, the same one where Professor Saeed served for 22 years, now looks after the Markaz affairs, being its vice-chancellor.

Saeed, however, will not speak of bin Laden even though he is an ardent supporter of the Taliban. He denies that the Markaz Dawa Wal Irshad was a foreign-funded project. He says the funds came from a group of affluent traders who had offered money to buy cheap farm land near a village, Nangal Saada (Muridke), about one km from the main Grand Trunk (GT) Road. A Saudi trader, Ahmed, contributed Rs 10 million (the same figure as Osama's) while another, Saudi Sheikh, donated more millions for the construction of Dawa Model School inside the Markaz premises. 'Generous donations' were also received to build an industrial home for female students inside the Centre.

The Lashkar, similarly, owes its existence to private donations. The Professor is at pains to deny the widely held belief that it is on the payroll of the Inter Services Intelligence, the Pakistani Intelligence agency that is seen by many as propping up the terrorist campaign on Kashmir. 'We do not get a single rupee from the government,' says the Professor.

Alongside the Markaz Dawa Wal Irshad, the Lashkar has grown from strength to strength. Today, it is one of the most active militant groups working inside Jammu and Kashmir, with operations based on the Pakistani side of the border. It has a growing base among the shopkeepers, lower-level bureaucrats, soldiers, and students in Pakistan.

It has also become deadly effective. The Lashkar leadership claims to have acquired Chinese anti-aircraft guns and 60 mm heavy mortars. 'Our cadres have procured the latest Chinese-made guns which can be used against fighter aircraft and to destroy bridges and buildings,' trumpets the Lashkar-e-Toiba mouthpiece, *Jihad Times*. The Lashkar also has heavy mortars that are accurate up to 2.5 km. These sophisticated arms have already been pushed into Jammu and Kashmir. The Lashkar does not lack communication lines either: militants use the latest technology to keep in touch with their commanders across the border.

The militant organisation reached this level of sophistication after receiving significant covert aid from the US Central Intelligence Agency (CIA) during the early 90s to fight off the Soviet invaders inside Afghanistan. The Professor has no qualms in admitting that he participated in the US-sponsored jihad against the Russians in Afghanistan. 'The US supported us with guns during Afghan jihad,' he says. 'If we were not terrorists at that time, then why are we terrorists now?'

Maybe because of Kashmir. The Professor likens the 'Indian occupation of the disputed territory' to the Soviet occupation of Afghanistan. For him Kashmir is a battlefield for jihad, a fifty-three-year-old 'custody battle', an open-and-shut case with Pakistan in the right. Not only does he want Kashmir to become a part of Pakistan, he also wants Pakistan to become a part of a global Islamic state – in the true sense. Because the Professor, an avid student of religion in college, believes that there is no Islamic government in the world. His worldview, knocked down into two basic sentences, is straight and simple: 'God has ordained every

Muslim to fight until His rule is established,' he says. 'We have no option but to follow God's order.'

The Professor is following God's order. And the instrument of God's order is jihad. The Markaz Dawa Wal Irshad website quotes a saying of Prophet Mohammad (Peace Be Upon Him) that elaborates its interpretation of jihad. 'Islam will live forever and for the sake of it,' quotes the website, 'a class of Muslims will continue jihad until the dawn of Doomsday. By means of jihad,' the site says, 'the Prophet spread light in the Arabian Peninsula. By dint of this factor of jihad, he captured even Qaisar and Kisraa. Keeping themselves on the same path, the followers of the Holy Prophet (Peace Be Upon Him) trampled under their feet the two superpowers of their time – Iranian fire-worshippers and Roman Christians. Hence, they raised the flag of the Quran and Sunnah so high.'

The Professor, undoubtedly, wants to do the same. His two main targets are India and Israel, Hindus and Jews, in that order, since they are the main enemies of Islam and Pakistan. A Lashkar-e-Toiba pamphlet titled *Why Are We Waging Jihad?* clarifies matters further. It establishes the Muslim right to revenge in history. Jihad is obligatory, it pronounces, for taking back Spain where Muslims ruled for 800 years. The same with Nepal and Myanmar. Of course, the whole of India, including Kashmir, Hyderabad, Bihar, Junagadh and Assam, also has to be retaken.

Thus, the attack on the Red Fort in Delhi is seen as a significant step in this direction. The Markaz website points out that the Fort was the symbol of Muslim power in the subcontinent and later the main target of the East India Company's machinations. It is also the site from where India's Independence day speeches are made on 15 August. The Professor confirms this: 'The *fidayeen* attack at the Red Fort was a symbolic activity [sic] intended to warn India that it should withdraw its forces from Jammu and Kashmir and stop the farcical show of talks.'

The Lashkar advocates the use of force in places like Palestine, Chechnya, Kosovo and Eritrea and has vowed that it would plant the 'flag of Islam' in Washington, Tel Aviv and New Delhi.

Ideologically, it helps that God's orders as believed by the Professor do not countenance democracy. 'I reject democracy. The notion of the sovereignty of the people is anti-Islamic. Only Allah is sovereign,' says the Professor. 'Democracy is a menace we inherited from an alien government. It is part of the system we are fighting against. Many of our brothers feel that they can establish an Islamic society by working within the system. They are mistaken. It is not possible to work within a democracy and establish an Islamic system. You just dirty your hands by dealing with it. If God gives us a chance, we will try to bring in the pure concept of an Islamic Caliphate.'

So, when it comes to the affairs of his organisation, it is the Professor, the faceless man of terror, who decides how many militants have to be sent to the Valley. But the Professor is learnt to have only a little know-how of ordinary weapons and has, so far, kept his distance from combat training. Surprisingly, the Professor has never been found involved in any act of violence or terrorism in Pakistan.

However, his decision to send in fighters is calculated on the number of deaths that have taken place and the requirement and capacity of the Lashkar-e-Toiba to absorb new fighters. The Lashkar and its political wing, the Markaz, have for many years been calling for the expansion of jihad to the rest of India to create two independent homelands for the Muslims of South and North India. As a first step, they had called for intensified activities in Hyderabad and Junagadh.

For the past couple of years, the Lashkar has been claiming responsibility for various acts of terrorism not only in Jammu and Kashmir but also in other parts of India. The Lashkar came into prominence with its much-trumpeted infiltration into Jammu and Kashmir in 1993 in collaboration with the Islami Inqilabi Mahaz, a militant outfit based in the Poonch district. Much before that, in the year the Markaz was founded (1989), a special training camp in the Kunnar province of Afghanistan was set up, reportedly in collaboration with the Afghan leader, Professor Abdul Rasool Sayyaf. The training camp was named Masada – the Lion's Dwelling.

The Kunnar camp took students coming out of the Markaz and trained them in military tactics. It served as a base to push thousands of committed youths to Kashmir.

The ongoing Lashkar operations in the Valley were reportedly given form at the annual convention of the Markaz in November 1993, when the Professor announced that Kashmir was the gateway to the liberation of Indian Muslims. The Lashkar had supplied cadre to the militant group, Al-Barq, earlier, but it launched its first independent operation in Jammu and Kashmir on 5 February 1993, with 12 insurgents attacking the headquarters of the 11 Jammu and Kashmir Light Infantry at Balnoi, Poonch. Two soldiers and three Lashkar-e-Toiba insurgents were killed in the attack. Since then, the organisation has been held responsible for hundreds of deaths and a large number of communal massacres in the State.

The Lashkar later shifted its militant operations from the Kashmir Valley to the Jammu region in 1997. Concomitantly, after 1997, there was a rise in militant activities all along the border districts of Jammu and Kashmir, particularly in the districts of Poonch and Doda.

The terror group also focuses on conducting a war of nerves. This, the Professor claims, has so demoralised the Indian Army that it has ended up using heavy fire, destroying its own buildings and causing the deaths of its own men in misguided attacks.

Analysts point to another factor behind the Lashkar-e-Toiba's success: the Punjabi base of the outfit. The Lashkar mujahideen mix easily with the local population of Jammu, who are linguistically allied to Punjab. Also, the Lashkar militants, unlike others, prefer to die in an encounter with security forces rather than get caught. For instance, in 1997, the largest group of militants killed in clashes with the security forces belonged to the Lashkar.

The Lashkar, however, claims that it can sustain such losses. About a hundred militants join the corps every month and a fresh batch of 'freedom fighters' queues up. The Lashkar-e-Toiba prefers not to reveal the exact number of militants it has currently deployed in Jammu and Kashmir. What is known, however, is that the Lashkar recruits and trains many more men than it actually requires for fighting in Jammu and Kashmir at any given time.

Compared to other similar organisations, the Lashkar has

proved to be a great success. Since its inception, it has managed to attract thousands of committed young men to its fold. The driving force behind its success in recruitment is deceptively simple. It uses its impressive organisational network, which includes schools, social service groups and religious publications, to create a passion for jihad. The Lashkar-e-Toiba has some 1,000 small offices all over Pakistan, which are supposed to recruit volunteers and collect donations for jihad.

But its militants are not sent to the war just to die as martyrs; they are trained to kill: trained in the use of infantry tactics and small arms – from handguns to assault rifles and rocket-propelled grenade launchers; trained in shoulder-fired Surface to Air Missiles (SAMs) like the Stingers; trained through a 21-day basic course called *Daura Aam;* and a three-month advanced course called *Daura Khas* geared towards guerrilla warfare which equips students for the use of arms and ammunition, and provides ambush and survival techniques.

The last page in the international edition of the Lashkar-e-Toiba's *Voice of Islam,* even teaches readers how to use swords, spears and daggers; how to set up an ambush and lay siege to camps and cantonments; and the rudiments of attacking the forces of 'disbelievers'. 'Learn all these things through the Holy Quran,' says the *Voice of Islam,* in its recruitment pitch for jihad.

The Markaz and the Lashkar-e-Toiba are extremely secretive organisations and take great care to conceal the identities of their office-bearers. For this purpose, they emulate the Palestinian organisations in the use of 'Kuniat', which are Arabic pseudonyms adopted from the 'Kuniats' of the Companions of the Prophet and later Islamic heroes. The followers of the Lashkar-e-Toiba come from all walks of life, from defence and nuclear establishments to industrial labour.

There are some distinguishing characteristics of the Lashkar-e-Toiba militants. They neither shave, nor have a haircut, allowing their beards and hair to grow long. They are taught to employ extremely cruel methods such as beheading victims who owe allegiance to the security forces and are non-Muslim. Like fighters of many other jihadi organisations, they generally wear *shalwars* that do not cover the ankles.

The Lashkar-e-Toiba is never short of manpower or resources because its affluent patrons, both internal and external, fund it generously. And though the Pervez Musharraf government has banned fund raising by jihadi organisations, the funds are still coming in.

That is because the Lashkar has innovated quickly. 'It costs millions to make a tank but only a few rupees to defend against it,' says an advertisement for the Lashkar, asking Muslims to pay for the mujahideen fighting in 'Held Kashmir' and Chechnya. The advertisement concludes with a borrowed reminder: 'If you are not part of the solution,' it says, 'you are part of the problem.' Even by Pakistani standards, the advertisement is direct. While many readers may have simply turned the page, a sizable number have not. Funding to the Lashkar has increased, mostly from Pakistanis, largely businessmen and those settled abroad, especially after the US attack on Afghanistan.

But Pakistan has begun to debate whether the government should allow religious groups to run their own complexes with large funding from abroad. Pakistan's Interior Minister Lt. Gen. (retd.) Moinuddin Haider says the government cannot take any action since no law has been broken. This position has changed since it has come under US pressure. He argues that most religious groups in Pakistan have their centres of activity, but that does not mean they are springboards for unlawful activity.

The actual springboard, the historical root of the militant organisation, was the Afghan jihad. The Professor's version of how the Lashkar was launched gives the whole credit to a Saudi national, Abu Abdul Aziz. Called an 'international soldier of Islam' by the Markaz and the Lashkar-e-Toiba, Aziz belongs to Hyderabad in India. He apparently went to Pakistan in the 1980s in connection with the Afghan jihad. He invited Muslims to join hands with him for launching an Ahle Hadith organisation. Aziz finally found the Professor and his companion Zafar Iqbal due to their Saudi links.

Abu Abdul Aziz started his career, says Professor Saeed, as a personnel officer with Saudi Airlines. During this time, the Afghan war broke out. Aziz quit his job and devoted himself to the jihad against the communist forces. Besides extending generous financial

assistance to the Afghans fighting the Russians, Aziz launched the
Muslim Jihad Organisation, with branches in Afghanistan,
Kashmir, Bosnia and the Philippines.

The version in the website, however, introduces another name
– a student named Abu Waleed Zaki-ur-Rehman. He 'went to
take part in the jihad in the Pakhtia province of Afghanistan'
and 'continued visiting the country (to) show the people the path
of jihad'.

This young man, 'fired with the zeal of jihad . . . met a
commander of jihadi forces . . . . Soon he was entrusted with the
responsibility of jihad. Mujahideen engaged in jihad under his
leadership . . . . He had the full cooperation of Arab mujahideen
who taught him the intricacies of jihad. From August 1987 to
January 1990, he continued his jihadi activities at the battlefront
of Kabul. At the same time, he stayed in touch with the Arab
mujahideen fighting in Afghanistan.'

The website adds: 'Around that time, Sheikh Jamil-ur-Rahman
declared an independent Islamic Emirate in Kunnar. Young Abu
Waleed and some other Pakistani Ulema (Hafiz Mohammed Saeed,
and others) laid the foundation of Maskar-e-Toiba in Kunnar, on
22 February 1990.'

The website exults at the Lashkar's role in sending Soviet
troops back to their country. 'On 14 February 1989, the Russian
forces were leaving Afghanistan in such a state that their
commander had to request the Afghan commanders that his forces
be allowed to leave unscathed,' it says. 'Then, a superpower, Russia
had to leave Afghanistan shamefacedly. Its defeat, on the one hand,
brought dignity to the Afghan nation, while on the other, it imbued
subdued nations with the passion for freedom.'

The website freely owns up to several attacks on Kashmir. But
the Kargil war is the moment it revels in: 'Around thirty-five
thousand Indian Army *jawans* were under siege. India's Bofors
guns were concentrated in one area which India was about to
lose. Pakistan was in a position to avenge the defeat of East
Pakistan, but suddenly the whole scenario changed. Prime Minister
Nawaz Sharif offered Kargil to India on a platter by signing the
Washington accord. It brought grave disappointment to the people
of Kashmir.'

'Be it the camp at Bandipura or the headquarters of 15 Corp Badamibagh, Red Fort at Delhi or the Srinagar airport,' the website boasts, 'the mujahideen have proved that no place on Indian soil was out of their reach.'

Such glaring admissions, followed by the attack on the Indian Parliament on 13 December 2001, provided the government with an ample opportunity to pressurise the US State Department for designating the Lashkar a terrorist organisation.

Another blow to the Lashkar came from the US in its post-World Trade Center phase. It froze all assets of the organisation. The Lashkar reacted by projecting an unfazed attitude. The mujahideen are its assets, it said, and they cannot be frozen.

Even last year, the US State Department, while issuing its annual report on terrorism, seriously contemplated declaring the Lashkar a terrorist outfit. Noted academic Selig Harrison, in an interview to a local Indian magazine, confirmed this. Harrison reportedly said that the US Justice Department had determined on November 2000 that the Lashkar was a threat to US national security and should be designated a terrorist organisation.

Key government agencies in the US, specifically the Central Intelligence Agency (CIA), objected, saying this would not be in the best interests of Washington. The CIA believed such a designation would threaten useful links with the ISI. The US further felt that such a step could embarrass General Musharraf. But after war clouds started gathering over the Indian subcontinent, following the closure of its airspace to Pakistan Airlines, among other steps, the Lashkar was finally stamped as a foreign terrorist organisation.

Diplomats in Islamabad believe that the change of heart on the part of the US was also due to the Indian Prime Minister's complaint to the US administration that 'Islamabad was involved in the threat to his life from the Pakistan-based Lashkar-e-Toiba.' Pakistan, however, dismisses Vajpayee's accusation. 'The accusation is baseless. Pakistan unequivocally condemns terrorism and threats of terrorist attacks,' Pakistan's foreign office spokesperson said in a statement early last year. 'We regret . . . that Pakistan has been accused of involvement in the alleged threat. The government of Pakistan holds Prime Minister Atal Behari

Vajpayee in high esteem and wishes him good health and a long life.'

Despite the war of words, the Professor himself realised they would soon be labelled terrorists. 'The Americans actually want to gain the Indian market. Besides, China is also a source of headache for the US. Therefore, it is hell-bent on heaping favours on India,' he says.

However, American pressure led the Professor to adopt a by-now familiar terror group tactic: change the organisation's name, drop the rank but keep the same role. So, he resigned as the Lashkar-e-Toiba chief after being at its helm for over 12 years. He insists that the decision was not taken under pressure and was finalised at a meeting of the Majlis-e-Shoora (Supreme Advisory Council) of the Markaz Dawa Wal Irshad. Incidentally, the Markaz is now called the Jamiatul Dawah and the Professor is its ameer.

Technically, Maulana Abdul Wahid of Poonch is the new Lashkar chief. He is at the head of a newly constituted 14-member general council. A majority of these members belong to 'Occupied Kashmir'.

Addressing a press conference in Lahore on 24 December 2001, the Professor talked about the changes in the Lashkar. First, he said, the Lashkar's activities would be confined to Kashmir and its offices had already been shifted there (apparently to cast aside suspicions regarding the Pakistani connection). This had been done, he continued, to counter 'Indian propaganda aimed at exploiting the situation in Afghanistan to its advantage. We want to block India from creating problems for Pakistan.'

Despite the changes, the Professor's beliefs remain intact. Talking about the function of the Jamiatul Dawah, he said: 'It is not essential for us to contest general elections. We reject the Western style of democracy. We only want reformation and don't believe in boundaries.'

'We have challenged the US authorities time and again to prove terrorism charges against the Lashkar-e-Toiba in any international fora. We repeat this challenge now. We can prove who is the real terrorist: India, Israel, US, Russia, or the mujahideen? The world fully knows who was responsible for the brutal killings of hundreds of thousands of innocent people by nuclear bombs.

Has the world seen a greater act of terrorism than that?' he asks. He sees the US as killing innocent civilian Muslims – and not for the first time. 'Thousands of tonnes of bombs were rained down on innocent Iraqis in 1991. Thousands of Iraqi children were deprived of their homes and were left to die in abject helplessness.'

The former Lashkar chief says he wrote to the US State Department to debate the issues and received a single-word reply: Thanks.

There is another cause that stokes the Professor's hatred for the US: Sheikh Omar Abdul Rehman. For the Professor, it is a matter of distinction that the Markaz Dawa Wal Irshad had hosted the famous blind Egyptian scholar. For the Americans, however, he is a man who masterminded terrorism in various parts of their country. A US court has already sentenced him to death. And the Professor is not too happy about that.

The Professor believes that America has underhand designs and that the operation against bin Laden is just its cover for occupying Pakistan. He says it is incorrect to consider the US a victim of terrorism. 'America had rained tonnes of gunpowder in different parts of the world unjustifiably, the latest being Afghanistan. The real issue before the US is not that of Osama; it actually wants to crush jihad in this region.'

The Zionists and the Hindus, he said, are perturbed over the resurgence of Islam through jihad and consider it a great threat. This lobby, he understands, has convinced America that an unchecked nuclear Pakistan would be the natural leader of the entire Muslim world. Professor Saeed, therefore, has given a call to the Pakistani nation to rise to the occasion, demonstrate total unity, and stop its rulers from taking a decision contrary to national sovereignty and solidarity.

In fact, Professor Saeed is a vocal critic of the military regime these days and insists that Pakistan should not have gone out of its way in cooperating with the US. According to the Professor, there is no logic in General Musharraf's argument that the US was allowed the use of Pakistani land and air space to safeguard the country's national solidarity. 'With this, we will jeopardise both our independence and our nuclear installations. The entry of American forces would facilitate any Israeli and Indian attack on our soil. The US must be kept away from this region,' he warned.

As for Osama bin Laden, he said, Pakistan should keep away from this issue. He stressed that the Muslim world must realise that the target of the enemy was not any particular area or country, but the spirit of jihad among the Muslims. The Lashkar-e-Toiba chief took special note of Iran's silence. He painted America as an aggrandising imperialist intent upon grabbing Muslim states one by one and said that the whole Muslim world must wake up to this danger. 'Instead of falling prey to the US designs, the Ummah should be prepared to face the challenge,' he says. 'The US, presently mourning the devastation of the World Trade Centre, would have to mourn much bigger losses.'

What about the 'losses' that the Lashkar has inflicted? There never were any, if you believe the Professor. It is all simply bad press and fabrication of stories. 'None of our activists was ever involved in the gruesome murders of the Sikhs in Chhatisinghpura and the brutal killing of the Hindu pilgrims in Pahalgam,' he clarifies. 'Even the Indian media has ruled out the involvement of the Lashkar-e-Toiba in these bloody acts of terrorism.' The Lashkar-e-Toiba, he informs, is not allowed to carry out any operation at public places. 'Its target is the Indian Army and its personnel who are trying to suppress the freedom movement.'

Interestingly, the former Director-General of the ISI, Lt. Gen. Mahmood Ahmed, who was removed on 8 October 2001 by General Pervez Musharraf, reportedly under American pressure, was seen as a supporter of the Lashkar-e-Toiba's jihad. General Mahmood, also considered pro-Taliban, reportedly attended the yearly conference of the Lashkar-e-Toiba held at Muridke from 13 to 15 April. The conference passed a resolution calling on its cadres in India to emulate the example of Mahmood Ghaznavi, capture Hindu temples, destroy the idols, and hoist the flag of Islam on them.

In November 2000, General Musharraf, under pressure from the Clinton Administration, did not allow the Lashkar to hold its annual conference at Muridke. A year later, anticipating no pressure from the Bush Administration, Musharraf allowed them to hold the deferred conference in Muzaffarabad, on the Pakistani side of Kashmir. When the Lashkar insisted on holding the conference at Muridke, the general was agreeable but reportedly asked Lt. General Mahmood to ensure that no journalists, Pakistani or foreign, would have access.

And yet, General Musharraf denies any links of the Pakistan Army and the ISI with the Lashkar or any other jihadi organisation. What's more, he denies their very presence in Pakistani territory. Major-General Rashid Qureshi, the media spokesman of General Musharraf and the Director-General of Inter Services Public Relations (ISPR), was quizzed on the point. He gave the stock answer: 'No group operating in Kashmir has any base in Pakistan.'

But there are dissenting voices. An issue of the Karachi-based English monthly, *Herald*, quoted Dr Khalid Mehmood Soomro, Secretary-General of the Jamiat-ul-Ulema Islam (JUI) based in Larkana, as saying: 'Why is the Pakistan army not fighting for Kashmir? Why are they getting our youth killed there? They are using our young men for their own goals . . . . Let's be clear on one thing. These jihadi groups can't function and survive without official patronage. Is there a single militant training centre in Pakistan which can operate without the consent of the Pakistan army? All militant groups are created and run by Pakistan's secret agencies. They have mobile phones, Land Cruisers and weapons. Where are they getting the funds from? Surely, it can't be all funded through public donations. Because if that were so, we would be getting similar donations, if not more.'

Ultimately, such voices don't matter. For the only voice the Professor is listening to is that of God. 'This jihad has been commanded by Allah Almighty,' he says authoritatively, 'and no one can stop it.'

The jihad rests in the Professor's hands. And don't forget – he is a very pious man.

'Assam's freedom is no wasted dream; it has a future and the struggle has just begun.'

Paresh Barua: ULFA

Subir Bhaumik

From the files of the CID, Assam Police:

CAUTION: This person is considered violent and armed.

Present Family Name: Barua; Forename: Paresh; Sex: Male.

Date, Place of Birth: 1 May 1957; Jeraichakali Bhariagaon, Chabua, Dibrugarh, Assam.

Also Known As: Paban Barua; Pradip; Nur-uz-Zaman, Kamruzzaman Khan.

Countries Likely to Be Visited: Bangladesh, Myanmar, Bhutan, Thailand, Pakistan, China.

Languages Spoken: Assamese, Bengali, Hindi, English, Naga, Chingfou.

Additional Information: Barua travels on a forged passport and identity card, lives on money obtained from extortion or robbery, and can handle all kinds of weapons. As a member of a terrorist organisation, he has procured weapons, ammunition, explosives and communication devices with money illegally obtained by the organisation.

Maximum Penalty Possible: Death.

Description: Medium build, fair, 5ft 8 in (173 cm), black hair, small but strong eyes and black eyeballs, a round nose and pointed eyebrows.

Distinguishing Marks: Cut mark on the right palm.

Characteristics: Reserved in behaviour.

Additional Information: Passed HSLC Examination, knows typewriting, worked as a railway porter from 1978 to 1982, worked as a mazdoor in the mechanical engineering branch of Oil India, Duliajan, for some time from May 1982. He is the self-styled C-in-C of ULFA. He has obtained arms and guerrilla training under NSCN, KIA, ISI of Pakistan. He always carries small arms. He ordered and approved kidnappings, killings, extortion and other violent

activities by ULFA and like-minded organisations in the State of
Assam and outside. He has been involved in incidents of kidnapping,
killing, extortion, bank dacoity, etc. He has established contacts
with foreign agents inimical to India . . . He is a member of
ULFA's Central Executive Council.

He rarely let down his team in a goalmouth mêlée or while negotiating a high cross or a flag kick. His sharp reflexes helped him save difficult penalty shots. His coaches and contemporaries are certain he would have played for India one day. But the anti-foreigner agitation that rocked Assam in 1979 took Paresh Barua away from the field of soccer to the world of guns.

Twenty-two years later, Barua heads the military wing of the dreaded United Liberation Front of Asom (ULFA). He still dreams of Assam's liberation and fancies himself as the Lachit Barphukan of his generation (the famous Assamese warrior who defeated the Mughals in the historic battle of Saraighat in 1672). His passion for soccer is undiminished, though now restricted to watching premier leagues on television. He remains a fitness freak and enjoys a quick game of chess, which he hates to lose.

But Barua is apparently in no mood to play games with Delhi. In India's troubled North-east, where most rebel leaders have called it a day and negotiated political settlements with the Centre, Barua is one rebel chieftain who has refused to give up. 'Assam's freedom is no wasted dream; it has a future and the struggle has just begun,' he told me during an interview on BBC World Service on 17 December 2000.

Leading the ULFA and ensuring its survival as an insurgent group has been no easy game for 44-year-old Barua, the same age as Osama bin Laden. He has thrice escaped capture or death when encircled by hugely superior Indian or Burmese forces. And, since December 2000, he has survived four attempts on his life by ULFA renegades and Bangladeshi mercenaries allegedly backed by the Assam police and Indian Intelligence.

The ULFA, though weakened by large-scale desertions, surrenders and casualties in encounters, has remained a fighting force capable of striking at specific targets. Barua's admirers and detractors alike agree that he is the one leader who has prevented the ULFA from falling apart. A senior Assam police official, reputed to be the mastermind behind the operations against Barua, said in an interview this year: 'Paresh Barua is the one man who has prevented the ULFA from coming to the table.'

Barua's firm stance has helped him retain the loyalty of hundreds of Assamese youths who continue to die for him. Many who have left him insist they still respect him but feel, as Luit Deury, the ULFA leader in-charge of the Bhutan base area, said in an interview on BBC World Service on 2 February 2001, that he is fighting 'a losing battle for a lost cause'. Says the ULFA's one-time publicity secretary, Sunil Nath: 'He has undeniable charisma. He is the one leader who is holding the ULFA together. The rest of the ULFA leaders are just useless.'

Barua belongs to a family of Matak tribesmen, known for their rebellious traditions. The Mataks fought the Ahom kings for several decades during the Moamaria uprising that shook the foundations of medieval Assamese society. Also, the village Barua hails from – Jeraichakali Bhariagaon in Upper Assam's leading tea-producing district of Dibrugarh – has a tradition of producing soccer stars.

Paresh Barua was sharp and intelligent at school, where he won a scholarship (britti). But his heart was in soccer. By the time he went to college, job offers were flowing in. He started by playing for Santipur Sporting, a first division club in Guwahati. Within a year, he was playing for Assam's junior squad. The Railways quickly signed him up as a porter. He served the Railways for four years (1978-1982) until he landed a better job with Oil India Limited. He played for the Assam seniors as well. Years later, in a newspaper interview with a Guwahati-based Assamese daily, Protidin, Paresh Barua fondly remembered his soccer days, his coaches and those he played with. 'One got the distinct impression that those were his best days,' reported the paper in 1998.

In 1979, just after the beginning of the Assam agitation, young Assamese men including Golap Barua, Arabinda Rajkhowa and Pradip Gogoi decided to form a militant organisation. They believed that the agitations by the All Assam Students Union (AASU) and other regional parties could not rid Assam of 'infiltrators'. Guns were needed to drive them away. So, on 21

April 1979, these young Assamese gathered at the ruins of the Ahom Royal Palace in Sibsagar and swore to liberate Assam by forming the United Liberation Front of Asom (ULFA).

The ceremony was simple but highly symbolic. The Ahom Palace, with its Rong Ghars (the central court), and Kareng Ghars (where festivals were held), represents the peak of Assam's medieval glory. Much of the distinctive consciousness of Assamese nationality has grown out of the legacy of the Ahom era. The Ahoms gave Assam a sense of territory and administration. They repelled the Mughals and prevented Assam's incorporation into an all-India empire. For the Assamese upset by the demographic changes arising out of the influx from Bangladesh or Nepal, the Ahom era is a throwback into an idyllic past. So, by forming the ULFA in the Ahom Palace, the young men emphasised their zeal to take the Assam movement on a militant course, beyond slogan-shouting street agitations.

Golap Barua alias Anup Chetia (now in jail in Dhaka) was a distant cousin of Paresh Barua, a fellow Matak from the same village. The militant face of ULFA was dormant after its formation, with the leaders merely holding regular meetings. By the end of 1980, ULFA leaders had begun using Paresh Barua's railway quarters for their meetings. But they only saw him as a useful sympathiser, not as a potential recruit. That upset the young goalkeeper. 'The ULFA leaders would keep me out of the house when they held secret discussions. Their attitude made me determined to join the ULFA and I became passionate for revolution,' Paresh Barua remembered later (in the BBC interview with the writer).

During the early years of the Assam agitation, the ULFA leaders did little by way of armed action. Arabinda Rajkhowa, Golap Barua and Pradip Gogoi were active members of the Assam Jatiyotabadi Yubo Chatra Parishad (AJYCP) as well. In fact, some of ULFA's founders like Bhadreswar Buragohain later reverted to overground politics. Buragohain joined the Asom Gana Parishad (AGP) in 1985 and became Deputy Speaker of the Assam Assembly. But as street agitations lost their course in the face of police action, a fringe group began veering towards militancy. Paresh Barua finally decided to leave Oil India Limited and take the plunge.

In fact, the holding of the state assembly polls amid much violence in 1983 was the turning point for many like Paresh Barua. 'By imposing elections that none wanted, the government turned democracy into a farce. It was [they were] polls with guns held on the head of the Assamese – which could not be accepted,' Paresh Barua said (in the BBC interview).

When a Congress government was returned to power in 1983, Chief Minister Hiteswar Saikia used a carrot-and-stick policy to subdue the agitation. He bought off some leaders while pursuing a tough line with the hardliners. That made the young Paresh, new to the ULFA, more determined to create a strong underground organisation. Within two years of his joining the ULFA, he had become the chief of its military wing. 'He was a cut above the rest of ULFA leaders. He worked hard and to a plan. He recruited the boys carefully and motivated them. Everyone knew he took the revolution seriously,' says Sunil Nath, the former ULFA publicity secretary.

During his very first year in ULFA, Paresh Barua started meeting leaders of other rebel groups in north-east India. Fraternal ties, he realised, would be the key to ULFA becoming a strong insurgent outfit. One such meeting with the General Secretary of the National Socialist Council of Nagaland (NSCN), Thuingaleng Muivah, was the most eventful. Until then, like most ULFA leaders, Paresh Barua was keener to drive out the 'foreigners' from Assam. Liberation from India was a stated but distant objective. But Muivah convinced Barua that there was no way 'foreigners' could be thrown out unless Assam became independent, with its destiny controlled by the Assamese. The meeting with Muivah, sometime in late 1983, also opened the 'Kachin connection' for the ULFA.

In late 1984, Paresh Barua led the first batch of ULFA rebels to the second brigade headquarters of the Kachin Independence Army (KIA), the largest rebel group in Northern Myanmar. This was located at Pasau in the southern Kachin hills, a good 50-day march from Assam's easternmost town of Ledo. The NSCN had put the ULFA in touch with the Kachin Independence Army. Twenty ULFA recruits were the first to undergo formal training in guerrilla warfare on foreign soil. This comprised three months of exposure to small arms and basic tactics. The training convinced Paresh Barua that more recruits needed to undergo it. 'No army can be built up without proper weapons and trained soldiers', he would say later.

Until then, the ULFA cadres could just about fire a revolver or lob a locally-made bomb. But with the return of the first KIA-trained batch, Paresh Barua had in place a small nucleus around which a force could form. He was determined to get more batches trained. The Kachin hills became for the North-east what Afghanistan was to be for the Kashmir jihad: a training ground for a number of rebel groups wanting to fight Indian forces.

But the KIA charged heavily. The first ULFA batch, however, was trained at a marginal cost because the KIA, as a 'fraternal revolutionary gesture', only charged for food and weapons. All batches to follow would have to pay in full. Paresh Barua, promoted as the ULFA's military chief, was suddenly in need of big funds.

The ULFA started committing bank robberies before it turned to organised extortion from big business, particularly tea companies. On 10 May 1985, Paresh Barua and other ULFA members carried out their first armed bank robbery, killing the manager of a nationalised bank branch at Silphukuri in Guwahati. They stole Rs 27,549 in cash and fled the scene in a vehicle forcibly taken from a hostage. Several offenders were arrested, the money recovered and a few weapons seized, but Barua could not be traced.

Providence came to Barua's rescue as well. Prime Minister Rajiv Gandhi initiated a fresh dialogue and signed the Assam accord with AASU leaders in 1985. Hiteswar Saikia was dumped and sent off to Mizoram as Governor. The AASU, which was fumbling under heavy repression, got a fresh lease of life. It rallied round other regional parties and formed the Asom Gana Parishad, which then swept the 1985 Assembly elections.

The 1985 elections also saw the emergence of the United Minorities Forum (UMF) organised by the Bengali Hindus and Muslims who felt threatened by the Assam accord. According to UMF leader Gholam Osmani, 'The UMF was a red rag to the Assamese bull and soon became an ULFA target.' Its general secretary Kalipada Sen was killed soon after the Assam elections, shot by ULFA gunmen at his Guwahati home in daylight. His colleagues were threatened as well.

The AGP's assumption of power gave the ULFA a much-needed shot in the arm. The state's security apparatus looked the other way as the ULFA began expanding its operations and became bolder by the day. Its leaders enjoyed the protection of AGP ministers. Paresh Barua disclosed during a recent BBC interview that the 'entire fund for sending the second ULFA batch for training in the Kachin hills came from the AGP government.'

During the training of the second, 60-strong ULFA batch, Paresh Barua again demonstrated he was better than anyone in the group. On their way back from the Kachin hills, the ULFA cadres were camping at the military headquarters of the NSCN at Chuiyang Noknu in late 1985. Two Burmese light infantry regiments attacked the NSCN base. Most ULFA men ran for cover, unaccustomed to such heavy combat. But Paresh Barua stayed on with the NSCN and fought. When the Burmese finally pulled back, Paresh was hailed as a hero. Assam's twentieth-century Lachit had arrived.

Investigations reveal that Rs 3.5 million were withdrawn from the Assam Police accounts reportedly by a senior AGP minister and made available to Paresh Barua, so that he could take the second batch of ULFA rebels to the KIA for training. Some senior police officials, without whose authorisation the secret funds could not be withdrawn, connived with the minister. Patronage, so essential for the growth of any militant outfit, was now available to the ULFA.

In the nearly five years of AGP rule (1985-1990), the ULFA grew into a hydra-headed dragon: its tentacles spread far and wide in Assam and some neighbouring states; its sympathisers were entrenched at all levels of administration and society, the number of its armed cadres swelling to around 2,000 at one stage. Its 'tax-collection machinery' was perfected with a near-accurate database. Those served 'notices' usually found their company balance sheets and income tax returns attached to back the demand. By the time President's rule was imposed on Assam in November 1990, the ULFA had set up a network of camps throughout Assam, a parallel administration and an extortion network never bettered by any rebel group in the region.

Paresh Barua was, however, not a believer in unrestrained terror. His military wing mixed selective terror with a Maoist form of rural populism. The ULFA, alive to its Maoist orientations, set up Unnayan Parishads (Development Committees), which would use government funds to expedite development projects.

The Unnayan Parishads would find out about the projects approved by the government, like the building of local roads and flood protection embankments. They would then force the local administration to place the money at their disposal by awarding the contract to someone recommended by the Unnayan Parishad. The ULFA would get the local population to provide free labour for the project. Token payments would be made and symbolic feasts organised to generate enthusiasm and support for the ULFA. Much of the funds for the project would go into the ULFA's coffers.

But anyone challenging the ULFA was firmly dealt with. Informers were given the harshest punishment, as also politicians opposed to the ULFA. Congress leader Utsavananda Goswami was 'sentenced to death' for allegedly fomenting communal riots in Gohpur in 1983. Tea firms and businessmen who did not pay up after receiving 'tax notices' were kidnapped, and even killed. Local officials who dared the ULFA were gunned down. Rhino horn smugglers were tried in 'people's courts for damaging Assam's natural wealth' and shot.

Two murders exemplified the ULFA's subtle but pervasive use of terror to secure the loyalty of the Assamese and force business houses and the local administration into submission. Surendra Paul, the chief of Calcutta's Apeejay Group who owned several tea gardens in Upper Assam, had been steadfastly refusing to pay, though the ULFA had agreed to negotiate on the demand. On 9 May 1990, as Paul headed for his gardens, after arriving at the Dibrugarh airport, ULFA men ambushed his convoy. Paul died in a hail of bullets.

Around the same time, the ULFA killed Dibrugarh's tough superintendent of police, Daulat Singh Negi, in a similar ambush. The killings threw the tea industry and the local administration into panic. The multinational firm, Unilever, was under demand to pay a few million rupees. It pulled out its executives from Assam on a day's notice, using a chartered aircraft flying out of the Research and Analysis Wing-managed airstrip at Doomdooma.

The killing of Surendra Paul and the much-publicised evacuation were, in some ways, a turning point for Assam. The powerful tea lobby started pressing for firm military action. Prime Minister Viswanath Pratap Singh could not upset Assam's ruling AGP, which was supporting his government at the Centre. But when Chandrashekhar ousted V.P. Singh, the Centre changed course rather swiftly.

Chandrashekhar was shocked at the state of affairs in Assam. Not only was the ULFA having a free run, but the Bodo agitation was also turning very violent. While the ULFA was beginning to control territory and dominate the state administration, resorting to a few select killings, the Bodos were freely using mass terror tactics, blowing up bridges, trains and buses. Hundreds died in the attacks.

It was later found that the Bodos had the support of the central intelligence agencies. The late Upendranath Brahma, at that time the president of the All Bodo Students Union (ABSU), admitted in an interview (at his Agartala residence on 21 December 1988) that 'all our boys are being trained by central government agencies in the use of explosives'. The support extended to the Bodo movement for a separate state – the Bodo slogan being to 'divide Assam fifty-fifty' – aimed to create enough chaos in Assam to justify President's rule which would, in turn, help rein in the ULFA. At least, that was Rajiv Gandhi's strategy. His honeymoon with the Assam student leaders, Prafulla Kumar Mahanta and Bhrigu Kumar Phukan, was over within two years of the Assam accord. He was convinced, by the end of 1987, (according to Amiyo Samanta, former Joint Director of the Intelligence Bureau), that the AGP was an 'anti-national (organisation) who [sic] deserved to be taught a lesson'. But before he could enforce President's rule, Rajiv Gandhi lost the 1989 polls and V.P. Singh came to power at the head of a coalition supported, among others, by the AGP.

If V.P. Singh had his compulsions to keep the AGP government in power, Chandrashekhar had none. Prodded by his junior Home

Minister Subodh Kant Sahay, Chandrashekhar was quick to act. President's rule was imposed on Assam on 27 November 1990, within six months of Surendra Paul's murder. Determined military operations in the Brahmaputra valley followed it up.

A senior AGP minister tipped off Paresh Barua about the impending Operation Bajrang. He had to organise a tactical retreat. Since the return of the second batch of the Kachin-trained guerrillas, the ULFA had set up a string of camps in Upper and Lower Assam. Some were as large as Saraipung (used as the General Headquarters or GHQ for military purposes) and Lakhipathar (used as Central Headquarters or CHQ for political purposes), where more than a hundred guerrillas could stay. These bases had been used for training fresh cadres and for political indoctrination. They were also used for holding hostages or those slated for execution.

All this went on with the full knowledge of the local police. Indeed, at Lakhipathar and Saraipung, the ULFA regularly played soccer and volleyball matches with local clubs, with Paresh Barua often in the thick of action. Then the Army swung into action. Barely 48 hours before the Army stormed into Lakhipathar and Saraipung, Barua had evacuated both the headquarters, avoiding any positional resistance. All senior leaders were given precise instructions about their escorts, the party shelter they would head for and their rendezvous points. Only token resistance was put up in some bases and approaches to camps were mined to delay the troops.

Bodies and skeletons recovered at Saraipung and Lakhipathar, provided the Army useful ingredients for its psychological operations or 'psyops'. But the ULFA was quick to recover from its reverses. The Army was desperate to find the elusive guerrillas they had seen on TV screens and magazine covers. But the ULFA was not confronting them. On the banks of the river Buri Dihing and then again at Kakopathar, the Army twice encircled ULFA units escorting Paresh Barua. On both occasions during the winter of 1990-91, the Army came close to nabbing him. But on both occasions, he fought his way out and melted away into the Assam countryside.

In the winter of 1990-91, the predicament of the Army was

quite similar to what the US faced recently in Afghanistan. It had the necessary manpower and firepower, but very little intelligence. The ULFA knew that positional resistance meant suicide, so it ran circles round the military positions, secure in the popular support it enjoyed and in its network of informers that was far superior to that of the Army. By a few select attacks on the troops, it provoked overkill, which could then be used to exploit Assamese sentiments.

The ULFA had sympathisers among the local civil liberties groups, the Assamese press and among urban professionals. Faced with a plethora of cases involving human rights violations, the Army was in a real fix. It was clearly losing the battle of hearts and minds. And it needed as much of a respite as the ULFA which was obviously under pressure, having lost its safe bases.

In June 1991, Operation Bajrang was suspended to create conditions conducive for an early election to the state assembly. The Army was also keen to review its strategy. With the suspension of the operation, the ULFA cadres came out in the open, visiting their families and friends and other comrades. Military intelligence agents trailed them and took note of their contacts, rendezvous and shelters.

By the time the elections were held, the Army was well prepared. It had slowly built up its own network of informers, even managing to plant some moles inside the ULFA, at least at the lower levels. The AGP lost the 1991 elections and the Congress returned to power. The ULFA's bete noire, Hiteswar Saikia, came back as Chief Minister. Having lost several relatives in ULFA attacks, he was determined to settle scores.

But Paresh Barua struck the day after Saikia assumed power. In a brilliantly coordinated operation on 1 July 1991, Barua's hit squads kidnapped fourteen senior officials, including Soviet coal-mining expert Sergei Gritshenko from various parts of the Brahmaputra valley. The serial abductions were aimed at two things: to regain the psychological advantage the ULFA had lost since Operation Bajrang, and to put the Saikia government on the defensive from the outset. Gritshenko was killed while reportedly attempting escape, while two ONGC engineers were killed when military units stormed rebel strongholds to rescue them.

But after playing it soft with the ULFA for almost two months,

during which he released a number of ULFA detenues, Saikia
suddenly turned tough. 'I am the Chief Minister of 22 million
people of Assam, not of 14 people, and I will not yield any more
ground to the ULFA,' he told journalists at a press conference. He
also started pressing Delhi for another round of military operations
to 'teach the ULFA a lesson'. (Quoted in Sanjoy Hazarika's
Strangers of the Mist, Viking, 1994.)

On 15 September that year, the Army was called out for a
fresh offensive dubbed Operation Rhino. This time, it was better
prepared. Within three months, many senior ULFA leaders were
arrested or killed. Paresh Barua's deputy, Hirakjyoti Mahanta,
feared for his ruthless killings, was arrested in an encounter on
the last day of 1991 and then killed in mysterious circumstances.
The Army says they shot him while he tried to escape; human
rights lawyers say Mahanta was shot in cold blood after extensive
interrogation.

With the Army in full cry, successfully regaining the military
space taken over by the ULFA since 1986, Hiteswar Saikia swung
into action, and tried to split the militant organisation. The central
intelligence established contact with the top ULFA leadership and
flew ULFA chairman Arabinda Rajkhowa, general secretary Golap
Barua and vice-chairman Pradip Gogoi to Delhi for talks.

Prime Minister P.V. Narasimha Rao was keen to negotiate but
only if the ULFA renounced violence and surrendered weapons.
The ULFA triumvirate was not disinclined but they wanted Paresh
Barua to agree, because he had complete control over the military
wing, despite the setbacks. Barua was in no mood for talks.

From his new-found base in Dhaka, Paresh Barua gave Swedish
journalist Bertil Lintner an interview which was published in *India
Today*. The interview asserted Paresh's 'determination to continue
the fight against the Indian state', and 'threatened severe
punishments for those betraying the cause of Assam's freedom'. It
put Rajkhowa, Golap Barua and Pradip Gogoi into a panic and
they talked the Indian intelligence into allowing them to go back
to Bangladesh to 'bring Paresh Barua out by convincing him of
the need for talks'.

But once they reached Dhaka, Barua put them under 'house
arrest'. Some surrendered ULFA sources say Barua severely

humiliated them. But Paresh Barua insists he managed to convince the three leaders of their 'mistakes' and motivated them to fight on.

Operation Rhino, preceded by Operation Cloudburst, deprived the ULFA of safe bases within Assam. The NSCN split in 1988, followed by violence between the warring Muivah and Khaplang factions, had also forced the ULFA to vacate their bases in NSCN-held areas in Burma's Sagaing Division. A new trans-border sanctuary was desperately needed.

During Operation Bajrang, ULFA had sent its foreign secretary Munim Nobis to Bangladesh. Nobis managed to get in touch with Colonel Farook, now convicted for masterminding the coup that led to the killing of Bangladesh's founder president, Sheikh Mujib-ur-Rehman. Through Farook's Freedom Party, the ULFA leader established contacts with Pakistan's Inter Services Intelligence (ISI) station chief based in Dhaka under diplomatic cover. In early 1991, the ULFA leaders visited Pakistan twice and secured a promise for help. But during one of those visits, Paresh Barua got into a major tiff with some ISI officials. He had been asked to avoid confronting the Indian Army and focus on sabotaging vital oil and defence installations. But he told the ISI officials that 'attacking the oil industry was out of the question as thousands of Assamese depended on it for their livelihood.' (Sunil Nath's recollections in *Strangers in the Mist*.) He would abandon this position a decade later.

By the end of 1992, Paresh Barua had set up firm relations with the Bangladesh military intelligence, the Director General of Forces Intelligence, and the Pakistani ISI. The ISI did not like Barua's independent attitude but were willing to open a 'second front in their proxy war' for unsettling the North-east. With the help of the DGFI, Barua was soon to establish a wide network of safe houses in Dhaka and Chittagong. He regularly visited Bangkok to establish links with an arms smuggling syndicate based at the Thai port city of Ranong.

One of his close lieutenants, Madhurya Gohain, was entrusted with smuggling the weapons bought at Ranong. The weapons would be loaded onto small vessels, which would sail to Wyakaung beach, south of Bangladesh's beach resort town of Cox's Bazaar.

ULFA cadres would carry them from there in small boxes to the Sylhet region and smuggle the weapons across to Assam via Meghalaya's Garo Hills. ULFA's initial arms purchases from the Kachins had cost Barua a fortune. Also, after the factional feud between the NSCN, the Kachin corridor was as good as lost to the ULFA. The alternate route was long and circuitous but easier to handle.

But safe houses in Bangladesh, though capable of sheltering leaders, did not form a good base area to launch operations in Assam. By the end of 1993, Paresh Barua, with the help of his lieutenants, Raju Barua (alias Cobra) and Luit Deury (now a surrendered militant), proceeded to set up a string of bases in southern Bhutan. According to one estimate, the ULFA now has at least 36 camps in southern Bhutan that, at their peak, housed up to 2,000 guerrillas according to Jaideep Saikia, Security Adviser, Government of Assam, in a paper, *Bhutan's Tryst with Assamese Separatism*, presented at the Institute of Conflict Management, Delhi.

These include its General Headquarters (used for military purposes) at Sukhni in Marungphu, its Council Headquarters at Dingshi Reserve Forest area, and a security-cum-training camp at Pemagetshel spread over the three villages of Khar, Shumar and Nakar. The base of the special strike force, *Enigma*, is also located at Deothang.

Some important ULFA bases in Bhutan are also at Mithundra, Gobarkunda, Panbang, Diyajima, Chaibari, Marthong, Gerowa, Melange, Dalim-Koipani (Orang), Neoli Debarli, Chemari, Phukatong and Wangphu. Most of the camps and other such ULFA establishments are in Sandrup Jongkhar, a district in southern Bhutan which borders Assam's Nalbari district. A straight road from Sandrup Jongkhar via Darranga-Tamulpur-Nalbari connects Bhutan with Assam's capital city Guwahati and other important towns of the state. Indeed, this road is the most strategic for Bhutan's east-to-west surface network and if the royal government turned the heat on the ULFA, this would easily be one of the first targets for the rebel group.

Though the royal government is pressing the ULFA to leave Bhutan, at least in a phased manner, the rebels are somewhat safe because the Indian Army has made it clear it would never cross into Bhutan on its own or in hot pursuit. The ULFA has extensive contacts in the Bhutanese administration built up by monetary favours. So it would likely be forewarned of any possible Bhutanese military action or a joint one involving Indian and Bhutanese troops (Mahesh Vij, GOC, 4 Corps, interviewed by Jaideep Saikia).

Paresh Barua displayed great strategic sense in creating base areas for the ULFA in Bhutan, considering the fact that Bhutan is heavily dependent on India. These base areas have helped him preserve the ULFA through the very difficult years since the beginning of Operation Rhino. As hundreds of cadres and leaders deserted the ULFA, Barua could still maintain the group's fighting nucleus intact in the jungles of south Bhutan. Despite reverses, the ULFA has continued to get recruits and funds. Its mass support base, though much eroded, has held up in many areas of rural Assam.

Paresh Barua's use of the media and other 'psyops' tactics also make for interesting study. This writer was intrigued at Barua's alacrity in admitting the loss of bases in the Assam-Bhutan border regions during the 1997–98 winter offensive by the Army, only to discover that a radio broadcast over the BBC (a bonafide news item and an exclusive one for the correspondent) was the quickest way for the chief to let his fighters know which bases had been lost and were better avoided. Some of his press interviews, always given over the phone, were clearly intended to prevent desertions or trigger off a political battle between rival political parties.

His Robin Hood image has also grown over the years. When approached by the wife of a senior engineer, Dilip Das, who had been kidnapped by the ULFA, Paresh Barua personally intervened to secure his release. The reason: Das's wife, Shyamoli, had called him brother. Barua, as it transpires, has rarely dishonoured a commitment given to a woman, like a good old Asomiya *dangoriya* (gentleman). This is in stark contrast to some of his subordinate commanders whose conduct with women has been unsavoury.

Much of the ULFA's political equations have changed over the years. It killed a large number of Congress leaders and candidates, including ministers like Nagen Neog, in the rundown to the 1996 state assembly elections. The AGP promised to address the question of Assam's 'self-determination' in its election manifesto, and ULFA expected it to function like its overground support group as during the 1985-1990 phase.

But once in power, Chief Minister Prafulla Kumar Mahanta pressurised the ULFA to start negotiations with the ruling United Front, which enjoyed its support. In 1997, the NSCN started negotiations with Delhi but Paresh Barua refused to come to the table. For him, talks had to address the question of Assam's sovereignty and had to be held in a foreign country under UN mediation. The other ULFA leaders, perhaps willing but incapable of defying Barua, were silent. An angry Mahanta responded by intensifying counter-insurgency operations under the newly created Unified Command. Paresh Barua would never forget this volte face.

On 8 June 1997, the ULFA's 'Volcano Unit' nearly blew up the Chief Minister's convoy and Mahanta had a narrow escape while on his way to offer prayers at Guwahati's Kamakhya temple. Two years later, in 1999, the same ULFA unit blew up Mahanta's number two man in the state cabinet, PWD Minister Nagen Sarmah at Nij Bahajani in Nalbari district. It then made unsuccessful attempts to kill two senior ministers, Zoinath Sarma and Hiranya Konwar.

The ULFA-AGP honeymoon was over. The AGP had been firmly co-opted by the Indian state and its leaders no longer pandered to ULFA's separatist designs. In every election, from the local village councils to those for Parliament, the ULFA unleashed rampant terror, killing political workers and leaders to ensure the defeat of AGP candidates. Hard pressed as never before, the rebels also started bombing vital installations like oil pipelines.

By 1997-1998, the ULFA's transition from a rural Maoist style guerrilla organisation into one that had come to depend on large-scale urban terrorism was complete. As it lost the physical space in Assam to an ever-domineering security apparatus, and faced large-scale desertions, the ULFA resorted to an ever-increasing use of terror to preserve its existence and keep the state at bay.

In the rundown to the violence it usually unleashes with other separatist groups in North-east India on the eve of the Indian Independence Day celebrations, the ULFA struck an oil depot at

Thekraguri in August 1997, and blew up rail tracks in several areas. Intelligence reports indicated that the ULFA had plans to blow up all the four oil refineries in Assam, ostensibly at the ISI's prodding. The Assam police responded by unleashing 'secret killer teams' made up of surrendered militants, who began to kill close relatives of several senior ULFA leaders like Arabinda Rajkhowa and Mithinga Daimary. The ULFA retaliated by firing rockets at a hideout of the surrendered ULFA militants (popularly known as SULFA) in Guwahati. They then assassinated Tapan Dutta who had once headed the ULFA's Dibrugarh district unit before surrendering.

The bloodbath degenerated to an unusual low, with relatives of both senior politicians and ULFA leaders becoming targets for the first time. Even as the factional feud between the ULFA and the SULFA worsened and military operations mounted, the ULFA hit back by attacking Army officers when they were off-duty. Two colonels were killed while visiting the Kamakhya temple in 1998; another killed while visiting an Assamese family during Bihu; a Central Reserve Police Force (CRPF) commandant was killed while visiting the Guwahati Zoo; and a Brigadier was killed in the heart of Guwahati while visiting a dentist. It was a ploy to restrict military officials to the barracks.

But the security agencies hit back at the ULFA by mounting a proactive policy of penetration and attack. On 29 August 2000, while the ULFA guerrillas led by their deputy commander-in-chief Raju Barua were preparing for an attack on a CRPF outpost at Bansberi in Barpeta district, two 'moles', Champak Patowary and Rocket Tamuly, fired on their comrades, killing and injuring many of them. Both were killed in a counter-attack by the ULFA but an injured Raju Barua had to abandon the operation.

It became increasingly difficult for Paresh Barua to run the show from Bhutan. Then, between December 2000 and September 2001, small teams of hired Bangladeshi mercenaries (belonging to the crime syndicate, *Seven Stars*) and the SULFA launched four attacks on Paresh Barua at his hideouts in Bangladesh. The first attack, on the Khagracherri-Chittagong road, misfired because Paresh Barua was not travelling in his vehicle. But the mercenaries nearly got him in the second attack when they fired on him as he came out of the Basin Leaf restaurant in Dhaka's posh Gulshan area. His goalkeeping reflexes saved him that day but one of ULFA's top financial fronts in Bangladesh, Sheikh Rumi, was killed. Three months later, the mercenaries planted a powerful explosive at the house of a Jatiyo Party (headed by former President Ershad) politician Abul Qashem and exploded it. But Paresh Barua had gone out to dine with a key contact and was saved.

And finally on the eve of the Bangladesh parliament elections, the mercenaries attacked Paresh Barua as he came out of the office of Challenger Transport in Dhaka's Segun Bagicha area. Again, Barua's razor-sharp reflexes saved his life and he fought his way out of the embattled area, vanishing yet again in his black Toyota Land Cruiser. Since these attacks, his regular telephonic contacts with pro-ULFA intellectuals, key overground sympathisers and some journalists (this writer included) dwindled. His personal security in danger, Barua was taking precautions. But he called this writer to wish him a Happy New Year in late December. Asked how he had been, Barua said, 'Not very well but not very bad either.' He took some interest in the way the talks between the Indian government and the NSCN were shaping up. And he was keen to figure out whether India and Pakistan would go to war.

Before the 2001 Assam Assembly elections, the ULFA unleashed a violent campaign against the AGP-BJP alliance. Paresh Barua was determined to square up with Chief Minister Mahanta and also keep the BJP out of power in Assam. Barua's detractors believe he has taken an anti-BJP and a pro-immigrant line to please his allies in Bangladesh and Pakistan. But those who have analysed the ULFA's political transition argue that it has consciously decided to project itself as 'a movement of all those residing in Assam.'

This stance could have grown out of the ULFA's military necessity to widen its support base and acquire multi-ethnic appeal.

But the ULFA's image took a considerable beating in late 2000, when its men were accused of resorting to mass massacres of Bihari, Marwari and other Hindi-speaking people. A hundred and eighteen people of these communities alone were killed in November-December 2000. (Compare this with the 116 people killed in all by the ULFA between 1986-1990.) Some suggest that the ULFA was trying to tie down the security forces in a static deployment mode. Others say there was a conscious attempt to link the Hindi-speaking populace with the Indian state and still others argued that the ULFA was merely acting in desperation, trying to undermine the AGP government in an election year.

But though the ULFA denied involvement in these massacres, the allegations have stuck. From the select killings of the pre-Bajrang era to the indiscriminate killings of late 2000, the use of terror by the ULFA has grown. Its financial resources, much depleted, are still considerable. It continues to get recruits – but just.

Much of this is still possible because Paresh Barua continues to keep the goal for the ULFA. The match has become dirty and there is too much foul play by both sides. But only a 'sudden death' can claim Barua – be it the mercenary's bullet or a sudden change of mind in a post-World Trade Center setting that might lead him to put down the gun and talk peace after a long, long time.

See two studies on the ULFA: Samir Kumar Das's *The ULFA – A Political Analysis*, Ajanta, 1994; and Udayon Mishra's *The Periphery Strikes Back*, Indian Institute of Advanced Study, 2000. Also see Subir Bhaumik's article *Northeast India: The Evolution of a Post-Colonial Region* in Partha Chatterji's *Wages of Freedom – FiftyYears of the Indian Nation-state*, Oxford University Press, 1998; and Jaideep Saikia's brilliant paper *Revolutionary or Warlord: The ULFA's Organisational Profile* presented at the Institute of Conflict Management, June 25-27, 2001.

'As long as the Sinhala nation is buried in the mud of racist politics, we have no alternative but to continue our struggle.'

Velupillai Prabhakaran: LTTE

R. Rajagopalan

The chiefs of the intelligence outfits of six countries had a quiet meeting in London in February 2000. On their agenda was the Liberation Tigers of Tamil Eelam (LTTE), a guerrilla force fighting bloodily for a separate Tamil heartland in Sri Lanka for the last three decades. That the organisation had come under such scrutiny testified to its lethal ability.

The intelligence chiefs also talked about the force behind it – the man who had formed the organisation in 1976 and turned it into a devoted band of soldiers for Eelam (the Tamil state). A militant leader who expected his cadres to prefer a cyanide capsule over capture or forced betrayal. Who is this man who commands such loyalty over life?

That question leads to the story of Velupillai Prabhakaran – parent, nurse, and God of the LTTE. To begin at the beginning: Prabhakaran was born on 26 November 1954, the youngest of the four children – two sons and two daughters – of a District Land Officer, Thiruvenkatam Velupillai (now living in Trichy in India) and his wife, Vallipuram Parvathi. It was a middle class family. Thiruvenkatam was a strict disciplinarian; Parvathi was deeply religious. Prabhakaran may or may not have exhibited fear at the sound of crackers as a child (as his mother told this correspondent) but there was no doubting that he was fired by a passion for restoring Tamil dignity and rights. When he was four years old, the 1958 riots occurred. Violent incidents of the racial discrimination between the Tamil and the Sinhalese were firmly implanted in his mind.

Prabhakaran, the favourite child of his father, did his first two years of schooling in Batticaloa. He was a mischievous and average student not interested in his textbooks. His father moved to Vellivetitural, a small coastal town of some 10,000 Tamils, a couple of temples and one church. Prabhakaran would often be by his father's side as he discussed Sri Lankan politics and the problems of ethnicity that defined it. But school failed to arouse young Prabhakaran's interests; the lives of Subhas Chandra Bose and martyr Bhagat Singh did. Books on Bose, the leader of the revolutionary Indian struggle for freedom were his favourite. He discovered as a schoolboy the delights of the catapult and preferred perfecting the art of shooting down objects to other sports.

Vellivetitural was the cradle for Prabhakaran and a nuclear model of Tamil society. It was here that a teenaged Prabhakaran had a foretaste of Tamil-Sinhala discrimination: one of his closest friends did not get admission to a Bachelor of Engineering course in the university of Colombo. It was provocation enough. Prabhakaran reportedly stole Rs 75 from a neighbour in Vellivetitural to help his friend. Prabhakaran also saw more discrimination. Tamil tea pluckers and fishermen bore its brunt. Even common goods like garlic and onion sold at exorbitant prices in the Tamil majority north-eastern province of Jaffna.

Still in his teens, Prabhakaran drifted, first, to the Tamil Student League (TSL) and the Tamil Youth League (TYL) that organised street protests. He participated in a movement led by a local leader, Dhanabhala Singham. Singham's protestors burnt a bus and the effigy of the principal of the university of Colombo. He also met the Tamil United Liberation Front (TULF) leader Dharmalingam. Soon, by 1972, Prabhakaran had formed the Tamil New Tigers, its initials, TNT, being an inadvertent clue to the more explosive organisation he was going to sire four years later.

By this time, Prabhakaran had a sure sense of direction. He would absent himself for days from his home and go around in shorts, meeting people and discussing politics. In 1972, he was wounded in the leg when a bomb he was making burst on him.

Three years later, Prabhakaran was accused of the murder of the Mayor of Jaffna, Alfred Duraiappah, of the Sri Lanka Freedom Party. It was said that a day before the assassination Prabhakaran had walked into a friend's house armed with a nearly rusted revolver. His ammunition was made from matchboxes, the tip of each match being patiently scratched out, made into pellets and used as explosive powder. On 27 July 1975 Duraiappah was shot as he was visiting a temple. According to LTTE lore, Prabhakaran, known to be an excellent marksman, had himself pulled the trigger. His legend was born.

The assassination made Prabhakaran famous. Suddenly, those in Jaffna knew of a group that called itself the Tamil New Tigers. Three of Prabhakaran's accomplices were caught; the man himself escaped. The police began a manhunt but Prabhakaran, acutely aware of any threat to his and his group's safety, took enough precautions. He avoided returning to his own place and slept at a friend's house. Prabhakaran was later acquitted of the murder charge when the LTTE owned up to the murder in 1978 – along with 11 others.

Duraiappah was Prabhakaran's first victim and his assassination marked the first military encounter in the militant struggle. He can also be seen as a political person whose death was the LTTE's first body blow to the political and social principles that defined Sri Lankan society. 'By the mid-1970s radicalisation of politics in Jaffna was an established fact,' writes Lankan historian Professor Kingsley de Silva, 'and with radicalisation came violence, including the beginnings of terrorism as a fact of life in the politics of the Tamils . . . ' The early targets were Tamils proximate to the government. Duraiappah was one such.

The political scene in the early 70s and 80s was one of authoritarianism. The ruling coalition, elected in May 1970, extended its five-year term by two years to 1977. The coalition kept invoking its emergency powers month by month. Secondly, the judiciary became nearly ineffective to check administrative abuse. To top this, the government institutionalised the preferential treatment of government supporters.

These factors added to the ferment of Tamilian sentiments. Tamils were increasingly being alienated from the Sinhalese since the new constitution was adopted in 1972. One result of this alienation was, in the words of Professor Kingsley de Silva, 'the conversion of a large section of the Tamils of the north to the idea of a separate state: it is an indication of the intensity of feeling in the Tamil areas at what they saw as a deliberate attempt to reduce them to subordinate status.' A Tamil United Liberation

Front (TULF) leader, S.J.V. Chelvanayakam, made the first public announcement for a separate Tamil state.

This same period, between 1976 and the early half of the eighties, was of growth and efficient networking for the LTTE as compared to the horrendous violence it unleashed in the following decades. In 1976, S. Subramaniam, who headed a small militant group teamed up with Prabhakaran. He would remain his most loyal asset, helping him out when he was arrested in Madras in 1984. On 5 March, Prabhakaran looted a bank of Rs 500,000 and jewellery worth Rs 200,000. The money helped found the LTTE and funded its training camps in the forest of Killinochi and the northern town of Vavuniya. Prabhakaran recruited and trained young men at Poonthottam, two miles from Vavuniya, and opened another training camp.

In 1977, Uma Maheswaran, secretary to the TULF's Colombo chapter, joined Prabhakaran. Maheswaran was older than Prabhakaran and was made the LTTE's *de jure* chief. But soon rivalry between the two caused the first split in the LTTE with Maheswaran taking away many rebels.

During this period, there was an exodus of the rebels from Jaffna. The Tamil rebels crossed the Palk Straits to India to dock in small ports like Nagapattnam (300 km from Chennai, formerly Madras) and Tuticorin. Nearly 300,000 to 350,000 Tamils crossed over to India during this time as recorded by the Indian government. As they gained asylum in India and elsewhere, their specific purpose crystallised into raising money for the organisation.

Until 1983, no Tamil militant group had its own boat. The 'boys' were ferried by boatmen who were masters of the Palk Straits. They knew the weather and the movements of the custom and navy boats and were indispensable, if unsuspecting, couriers transporting LTTE cadres into Tamil Nadu. Each ride to Tamil Nadu cost anything between Rs 100 and Rs 200, though some did the favour free.

The exodus from the North-eastern province of Sri Lanka in the eighties paid rich dividends to the LTTE by the help received from the many engineers and white-collar workers who went to Europe. A skilled work force was available to the organisation and that too in areas where it could spread its sphere of influence without fear of quick detection. The extent of the LTTE's network and expertise grew.

The pro-LTTE Tamil network was also very effective and was able to steal software from the Pentagon that could show simulated views of as many as 350 airports in the world capitals. Today, the software is widely available but when it was smuggled out in 1988, it must have been a real find.

When the militant organisation was founded, its name was Liberation Tigers. It was christened as the LTTE when the tiger was chosen as its symbol. Its logo showed the head of a roaring tiger, paws outstretched, with two rifles and 33 bullets set against a circle ringing the tiger's head. Historically, the symbol can be traced to the imperial crest of the Cholas, the Tamilian dynasty that ruled India from the 11th century. For Prabhakaran, the tiger stood for Tamil resurgence and cat-like guerrilla warfare. The LTTE chose the name 'Tigers' in contradistinction to the lion, the symbol found in Sinhalese history. In the jungle of civil war thus, the struggle is between the Sinhalese lion and the Tamil tiger.

The Sinhalese take pride in the lion as a symbol and have made it a prominent feature of Sri Lanka's national flag which is made up of three coloured sections. The green represents the Muslim population; the orange represents the Hindus; while the biggest part dominated by red represents the Buddhist Sinhalese population.

The LTTE, on the other hand, prides itself in the tiger and its most famous group of fighters takes its name from the symbol. Called Black Tigers, it is an elite suicide squad of commandos. The Black Tiger is the most coveted grade that a Tiger or Tigress recruit aspires to. Prabhakaran handpicks the Black Tigers after they pass through an advanced commando course. They form the LTTE's death squad and are responsible for the peculiar kind of assassination the organisation has come to specialise in: the human bomb. A person with a bomb, strapped to his body, is detonated near the target. A prime example is Rajiv Gandhi's assassination in 1991 that killed 18 people including his female assassin and seriously injured 44.

It is not Black Tigers alone; all Tigers and Tigresses are able to steel themselves for death. Most bite into their cyanide capsules – handed out to them when they are passing out of training – when capture is imminent, a point underscored by the fact that only a very small number of Tigers and Tigresses are ever captured alive by the Sri Lankan security forces. The idea had perhaps come to Prabhakaran when Sivakumaran, a Tamil youth hero, had committed suicide.

Prabhakaran believes it is discipline that leads to such death-defying loyalty. Hard military training and LTTE ideology are, therefore, dinned into the recruits. Their life is truly spartan. They cannot smoke, drink, or have sex. Indeed, the last was what reportedly caused the split between Prabhakaran and Uma Maheswaran. A rifle and cyanide vial, a change of clothes, and a pair of slippers are the Tigers' material possessions. They have no relations outside of the Tigers, having renounced family ties, friends, and material pleasures. What they have in abundance is devotion to the idea of a Tamil state and to-the-death loyalty for Prabhakaran. Prabhakaran has ingrained such abiding loyalty in his cadres that the organisation has, as a whole, carried out at least five times more suicide attacks than other similar organisations put together.

Indoctrination mainly consists of propaganda against the Sri Lankan army, detailing its 'atrocities'. It can be subtle and emotive. The speech Prabhakaran gave on his birthday in 1992, the year after Rajiv Gandhi's assassination, exemplifies the tone of deliberate and careful denunciation. Similar thoughts have marked his subsequent speeches.

'From the strategy of the government we must be quite clear about one thing. That is, there has been no change in the hegemonic attitude of the Sinhala-Buddhist chauvinism to dominate and rule over the Tamil nation by armed might. As long as the Sinhala nation is buried in the mud of racist politics, we cannot expect a fair and reasonable solution from the Sinhalese ruling class. Our people should realise this bitter political reality . . . . Our enemy is heartless and committed to war and violence. His objective is to destroy our homeland. We cannot expect justice from the magnanimity of his heart. What can we do in these circumstances? We have no alternative other than to continue our struggle, to continue to intensify our struggle . . . .

'But our enemy is committed to violence. Therefore, he has imposed an unjust war on us. Today, the enemy's armed forces have come to our doorstep and are beating war drums [sic]. They are bent on devouring our land and [seek] to destroy us. He [the enemy] is prepared to shed any amount of blood in this genocidal war.'

On the one hand, the enemy is pointed out and hate is cultivated towards him. On the other, Prabhakaran is given a complete image makeover and the recruits made to venerate him. In the carefully groomed image of Prabhakaran prepared for consumption by the recruits, he fits many roles. He is an incorruptible person, the man with the Eelam mission, the heroic fighter, the skilled guerrilla, the fatherly overlord of the recruits – it is the theory of paternal dictatorship with a sinister twist.

Prabhakaran too reciprocates the loyalty he receives in full measure – at least, he is careful to be seen reciprocating it. The LTTE chief named his first son Charles Antony, after his right-hand man, Charles Lucas Antony (also called Seelan). Charles Antony was the most high-profile hit man in the LTTE. To him goes the credit of staging the first ambush by any militant group on the Lankan army in which two soldiers lost their lives. While Prabhakaran was in India, Charles Antony was the man in command in Jaffna.

He led from the front one of the most ambitious of the LTTE's attacks on the Sri Lankan police. Eight armed Tigers burst into the well-guarded Chavakachcheri police station taking the police personnel by surprise. Police officers were shot at and communication sets destroyed. The police station was overpowered. Such was the impact of the LTTE attack that the police force closed down eleven outlying police stations in Jaffna. However, in the thick of action a bullet hit Antony on the kneecap.

On July 1983, the injury proved to be a fatal handicap. A posse of police officers surprised Charles Antony while he was having coconut water with friends in a village ten miles from Jaffna. The LTTE hit man fled into the accompanying rice fields but his injury slowed him down. The police closed in. Sure of his fate if the police captured him alive, he asked his friend to shoot him.

The Sri Lankan forces found his body amid the fields. When it was identified, they had reason to be happy – the number two man in the LTTE had been struck down. Little did they realise that Prabhakaran would take brutal revenge.

He staged an ambush that marked the end of the LTTE's relatively dormant 1978–1983 phase. On 23 July 1983, LTTE militants fell on an army patrol at Tinnevely in Jaffna peninsula, killing 13 soldiers. It was a meticulously planned operation in which all of the LTTE's top brass took part.

An army patrol of about 15 men in a convoy was slowly approaching Tinnevely at night and reached a narrow road that the militants had mined. The jeep was thrown off the road as the mines exploded and the Tigers fired at anything that moved. The LTTE militants were jubilant until they learnt that one of their foremost lieutenants had also died. It was a hard blow. It was imperative for them to flee the scene of the ambush – one soldier had managed to escape and would obviously relay the news – taking the bodies of the soldiers and their fallen comrade with them.

The bodies of the soldiers were later found mutilated. The viciousness of the ambush sparked the anti-Tamil violence of July 1983 that killed approximately 600. The brutal reprisals of the LTTE do not target only the Sri Lankans. They fall as bloodily on those who stray from the Tigers' strict code of conduct. If discipline instils loyalty, fear keeps it in line. Serious offences like rape, murder, and acceptance of bribes meet with a quick death. It is the same with betrayal. Only peccadilloes escape the extreme penalty. Public humiliation, generally in the form of a tongue-lashing, is often their punishment.

In its unending battle for Eelam, one recurring period, the fourth week of November, finds the LTTE speaking out loudly. The Sri Lankan intelligence agencies as well as the Indian Research and Analysis Wing (RAW) and the Intelligence Bureau (IB) invariably give warnings related to this period. The only two other forecasts that the IB and RAW periodically make are the January 26 and August 15 intelligence briefs. The fourth week of November, however, is *Maa-Veeran vaaram*, the Supreme Hero's week, the week of Velupillai Prabhakaran's birthday on November 26.

For LTTE cadres, November 26 is Hero's Day. In fact, the death count is high during every fourth week of November in the southern provinces of Sri Lanka because the Sri Lankan forces attack the LTTE to demoralise its ranks.

Prabhakaran, however, considers the birthday an unlucky day. He usually spends it in non-military activities. Apart from his suspicions relating to November 26 and the number 8 (the digits of the number 26 add up to 8), Prabhakaran is a devout Hindu. He believes, especially, in Kali, the Mother Goddess who combines in her aspect the creative and destructive attributes of supreme authority. She is a deity who embodies ferociousness. Her visage is black, her long hair is smattered, her tongue is out, and she wears a garland of skulls on her neck. She holds a decapitated head in her hands, has a large circular dot of *kumkum* on her forehead and rides – significantly – on a tiger. She symbolises the death of evil; she is the avenging force of good. Prabhakaran is reported to hold the same reverence for his mother.

Prabhakaran reportedly never initiates an assassination – including those of Rajiv Gandhi, former Sri Lankan President Ranasinghe Premadasa or the late Sri Lankan defence minister Ranjan Wijayaratne – without worshipping the Devi. In this he reminds one of the 17th-century Maratha warrior Shivaji. He was a worshipper of the Mother, and he too was a guerrilla fighter, heading a force that aimed to rid itself of Mughal sovereignty. However, he was never senselessly violent.

Prabhakaran prefers action to ideology. His little interest in reading stretches only to military matters. He has no interest in the intricacies of ideology and has often left that to Anton Balasingham, the London-based international head. He is a practical man, determined to nurture and toughen his group. His loyalty is with his cause and those who support it. The 1992 speech on his birthday succinctly introduces some of his firebrand ideas. Freedom is apparently dear to him and of the highest value. It forms the cornerstone of his speech: 'Freedom is a noble ideal. It is the highest virtue in human life. It is the basis for human progress and development. It is freedom which gives meaning and wholeness to life. The yearning for freedom arises as the deepest aspiration of the human spirit.'

This yearning for freedom is confronted with oppression. 'Human beings enslave human beings. They destroy each other. They exploit each other. Man has become the foremost enemy of man. Righteousness is undermined when one infringes on the human world. As a consequence contradictions emerge in human relationships in the form of caste, class and race.'

Human beings then struggle to emancipate themselves from 'the structures of oppression' that house the above contradictions. In fact, 'the innumerable struggles, revolutions and wars that erupted on the face of this planet for centuries are none other than the manifestations of the human passion for freedom.' Indeed, 'as long as there is oppression and injustice, as long as there are people deprived of freedom, there will be liberation struggles. This is the law of history. The motor of history is propelled by the human will to freedom.'

The will to freedom is paramount and so is the struggle that aims to achieve liberty. It co-opts every other aim or, indeed, personal ambition. So, LTTE warriors are required to become renunciants of a rather peculiar sort: they break away from those human relationships that have fostered them since childhood – their parents, close relatives, children – and swear off any digression from militancy whether it be sex or alcohol.

But Prabhakaran has exempted himself from the rule of observing celibacy without incurring any protest. In fact, he discourages any questions regarding his marriage and women in general. In the mid-1980s, he married a young girl who was on a fast-unto-death agitation against the Sri Lankan government. The woman was among nine students of the Peradeniya University at Kandy sitting on the strike that had been called to protest against the lack of security for Tamil students in the universities of southern Sri Lanka. The Tigers abducted the students as at that time the organisation was against hunger strikes and took them to Chennai on boats. Prabhakaran apparently met his future wife in Chennai. Today, he has two sons and one daughter.

His passion remains the cause of Eelam. For that cause, the LTTE guided by Prabhakaran has murdered pacifist leaders of the pro-government TULF who pressed for a negotiated settlement to the drawn out civil war. One of these killings showcases the LTTE's methods.

Two Tigers had earned the trust of TULF politburo member Y. Yogeswaran by frequenting meetings between the two groups. On 13 July 1989, both militants were joined by another from their ranks. They came to meet Yogeswaran at his house. He asked his security guards not to frisk them. One militant stayed at the gate while two went inside the house. TULF president M. Sivasithamparam and leader Amrithalingam, known as the general or 'thalapathy' of the Tamil struggle, joined the meeting. Yogeswaran's wife, Sarojini, was serving tea when the two Tigers fired, killing Amrithalingam and Yogeswaran.

The reason for the kill? A month earlier, Amrithalingam had spoken in the Sri Lankan Parliament pleading for the continued presence of the Indian Peace Keeping Force (IPKF) in the island. A decade ago, the Tigers were thought and seen to be sympathetic to the TULF. But then the LTTE began to overshadow the organisation. Those who had voted for the TULF had begun to believe that it was just opportunist. Quite glaringly, it accepted the proposal for a national government in 1982 though the government of the day used the idea to extend the life of Parliament for six more years. Soon, the TULF was seen as having let down the Tamils.

Another organisation that the LTTE had fallen out with was the Tamil Eelam Liberation Organisation (TELO). Prabhakaran had approached the TELO after the LTTE had been neatly split by the rivalry between Uma Maheswaran and him. The split had hurt the LTTE. Prabhakaran was made responsible for TELO military training. He used the time to regroup, getting back old LTTE hands and friends, and rebuilding an armoury.

On 25 March 1981, the TELO pulled off a big heist and was richer by Rs 8.1 million. A police crackdown followed immediately. Two senior TELO leaders were arrested. This was poll time for Sri

Lanka: it was heading for the District Development Council elections on June 4. At the same time, Uma Maheswaran decided to wreck the elections as the TULF had decided to participate in them. Maheswaran's group went violent and the police responded with real terror.

The heat was on, the booty acquired from the bank heist was gone with the TELO arrests and the LTTE found the going tough. Prabhakaran moved to Tamil Nadu. Lacking any money whatsoever, the group around him lived on survival rations.

The tie-up between the two militant groups lasted until the beginning of the eighties. By 7 May 1986, the state of affairs was such that the LTTE had hunted down and shot dead the charismatic TELO leader Sabarathnam at a betel plantation in Jaffna. Then, it executed several hundred TELO militants. At that time, the LTTE believed the organisation's proximity to India threatened its hegemonic vision of an independent Eelam. This Eelam would be a single-party Marxist state. And that single party would, of course, be the LTTE.

In pursuit of this vision, Prabhakaran has shown no mercy. Death is at his beck and call. Reportedly, he decides who is to be killed, and who should be on the LTTE's hit list. His criteria are simple: a person earns a mention in the hit list if he/she (a) is against the LTTE; (b) is pro-Indian; and (c) is a rival.

Even those who have defended the LTTE are not spared. The smallest deviation from an LTTE-always policy can bring death. A case in point is S. Nadaraja who had been LTTE's lawyer in the 1975 Jaffna Mayor assassination case. He had defended the LTTE ably. But the LTTE killed him in cold blood simply because he had participated in the IPKF-organised Indian Independence Day celebrations.

The IPKF was *the* bugbear of the LTTE. It was a visible target of the LTTE's animus towards India and its presence in Sri Lanka led to a chain of events that culminated in the assassination of Indian Prime Minister Rajiv Gandhi at an election rally in India in May 1991.

Four years earlier, when the Indian peacekeeper-soldiers arrived in Sri Lanka, the mood could not have been different. Tamilians greeted IPKF as deliverers. Within months, the relationship soured.

The Indian Peace Keeping Force had arrived under an agreement signed by Sri Lankan President Jayawardane and Prime Minister Rajiv Gandhi. Prabhakaran, heli-lifted from Jaffna, was in Delhi at the time. The LTTE supremo had a meeting with Rajiv Gandhi at his residence, 7, Race Course Road. Yet, even then he was quite suspicious of the Indians' intentions.

An intriguing episode took place. Prabhakaran refused to hand over his cyanide capsule and the bullets strapped around his waist. The Special Protection Group (SPG) and Intelligence Bureau were only trying to be careful. Prabhakaran, on the other hand, argued that without a pistol he could hardly use the bullets to kill Rajiv. Finally, Prabhakaran agreed to hand over the cyanide vial. On their part, the SPG reportedly agreed to let Prabhakaran in with bullets in his pocket. The LTTE chief agreed to go along with the accord but he was reportedly not happy with his incarceration in the government-run Ashoka Hotel.

One of the mandates of the IPKF was to disarm LTTE militants. The LTTE accused the Indian peacekeepers of committing atrocities in the guise of this mandate. Hostilities between the two began. The flashpoint occurred in October 1987 when the Sri Lankan navy intercepted a vessel carrying 17 LTTE militants. The LTTE appealed to the Indian government for their release but in the end 12 of the guerrillas had committed suicide. The incident provoked Prabhakaran. In a counterattack, LTTE commandos captured a ship carrying provisions for the army. In the ensuing battle, 11 Indian soldiers were killed.

But, Prabhakaran had been critical of the Indo-Sri Lanka accord even earlier. He addressed a meeting on 4 August 1987 criticising the agreement and the Sri Lankan government that was described as a 'Sinhala racist government'. Yet, he spoke of believing in the Indian Prime Minister, saying: 'The Indian Prime Minister offered me certain assurances. He offered a guarantee for the safety and protection of our people. I do have faith in the straightforwardness of the Prime Minister and I do have faith in his assurances. We do believe that India will not allow the racist Sri Lankan state to take once again to the road of genocide against the Tamils. It is only out of this faith that we decided to hand over our weapons to the Indian Peace Keeping Force.'

Two years later the Indian political scene and that position were changing. Rajiv Gandhi was defeated in the polls and Vishwanath Pratap Singh came to power at the head of a coalition in 1989. The process of the deinduction of the IPKF accelerated under him. The LTTE's viewpoint in that period can be gauged from an editorial in its official publication, *Voice of Tigers*: 'LTTE representatives . . . are firmly convinced that the Tamil Nadu government and the new Indian administration are favourably disposed to them and the V.P. Singh Government will act in the interests of the Tamil-speaking people by creating appropriate conditions for the LTTE to come to political power in the North-eastern province.'

India, in the grip of political instability, witnessed yet another change. Chandrashekhar became the Prime Minister with yet another coalition stumbling through the affairs of governance. Through most of this period, for a long 32 months in fact, Prabhakaran had gone underground. He emerged – at least in the newspapers – on April 1990. He was quoted in a newspaper as saying: 'We are not against India or the Indian people but against the former leadership in India which is against the Tamil liberation struggle and LTTE.' Now, that sentence may almost be read as a death warrant on Rajiv Gandhi.

The assassination helped the LTTE achieve international infamy. Prabhakaran was not innocent of the merits of having an international presence. It was at his behest that two World Tamil Conferences were organised in 1988 and 1989 in London.

Funds for the organisation came from those Tamils who had been granted asylum in countries of Europe. They worked hard, became rich, and created a corpus fund for the LTTE out of their savings. During investigations into the Rajiv Gandhi assassination, the CBI had to send letters rogatory to at least 26 countries – so wide was the LTTE network. The letters probed the LTTE's sources of arms, ammunition, ships, and even aircraft.

Perhaps it was at this time that the LTTE allegedly began to get into drug smuggling to raise funds. Though it denies the accusation it must be noted that the group has no compunction in training women and children as lethal guerrillas. Intriguingly, Prabhakaran – his worship of Kali has already been mentioned –

venerates women. He told this correspondent in Chennai, he is conservative in that he believes women should not be going out to earn a livelihood. At the same time, he holds that women have more will power to withstand crises: that is why he did not let Sivarasan, the mastermind behind the assassination of Prime Minister Rajiv Gandhi, witness the gruesome killing.

Prabhakaran's method has been to eliminate a leader at a crowded public place using a human bomb and, later, the remote bomb. For the actual assassination attempt, he uses highly motivated cadres. Dhanu, the Tigress who detonated a belt bomb attached to her person to assassinate the Indian Prime Minister, was one such militant. She had a reason to kill: it is alleged that the Indian peacekeepers were responsible for molesting her sister. Apparently, the feeling of outrage this must have caused had been worked upon.

Emotionalism is, indeed, part of a successful terrorist's game plan. To rouse his cadres, Prabhakaran has often resorted to conducting memorials for those who had 'sacrificed' their lives for the cause of Eelam. In his birthday speech in 1992, Prabhakaran exhorted his cadres thus:

'In our homeland, in the course of our struggle, extraordinary sacrifices have been made which have not taken place anywhere, at any time in the history of the world. I can proudly say that none can equal our martyrs in their dedication, deep commitment to the goal and tremendous courage that transcends the fear of death. Such magnificent qualities have enabled them to create an unparalleled legend of heroism. Our struggle, evolved through these remarkable feats of self-sacrifice, has become a guide and a driving force to the oppressed people of the world. The strength of our struggle arises from the fierce determination of our fighters. Their firm commitment and their courage to act without the fear of death are the force and resource of our struggle . . . . Our martyrs are the pillars of our freedom movement, whose blood enriches the history of our freedom struggle, whose ideal makes our struggle supreme, whose sacrifices shape the formation of our nation, whose memories make our determination stronger. We salute our martyrs who are the architects of the freedom of our nation.'

The architecture of this freedom struggle is self-admittedly bloody. According to the rough estimate of an Indian intelligence agency, between 1976 and 2001 the Liberation Tigers of Tamil Eelam have killed 12,500 Sinhalese, inclusive of defence personnel; 8,500 Sri Lankan Tamilians in Jaffna and the Northern Province, and 850 IPKF soldiers (official number by the Indian government). As recently as November 2001, a news agency came up with a staggering number of the victims: 60,000 killed in the civil strife since 1972.

The LTTE has also suffered. The Sri Lankan Army believes that more than 2,000 LTTE cadres died in the battle for Jaffna, which raged for 50 days from 17 October to 5 December 1995. The defeat ranks as the worst for Prabhakaran in the LTTE's 20-year war and was a considerable achievement for the Sri Lankan Army. It starkly pointed out that Prabhakaran could not defend the capital city of Eelam (Jaffna) and shamed him in front of the Tamil people.

The armed forces captured Jaffna despite an incredible LTTE campaign to distract them from this operation. This included attacks on the Kolonnawa and Orugodawatte Ceylon Petroleum Corporation oil storage tanks in Colombo on 20 October in which 23 soldiers lost their lives. A bomb attack on the army headquarters in Colombo killed 12 civilians. Black Tiger squads spearheaded both moves. The LTTE even indulged in massacres. Nearly a hundred Sinhalese men, women, and children lost their lives in border villages in both the North and the East.

On 5 December 1995, three days after Jaffna had been regained, Sri Lankan's Deputy Minister of Defence Anuradha Ratwatte ceremonially raised the lion flag over Jaffna city in front of thousands of troops. The event was broadcast live on Rupavahini television for the nation. Sri Lankan President Chandrika Kumaratunga was jubilant. She held a grand investiture ceremony for Ratwatte and conferred on him the rank of general.

Since that day, the ruling dispensation in Sri Lanka has considered 5 December particularly auspicious. According to a RAW intelligence report, this is the prime reason that the date for polls in Sri Lanka was the same in 2001.

Yet Jaffna has been just the one triumphant victory for Sri

Lanka's ruling elite over the militants. Prabhakaran, the Most Wanted, continues to remain elusive. He has only been apprehended once, that too in Chennai in 1993. It was an intriguing episode that brought out the extent of support for the Tamil fighter in Tamil Nadu.

Prabhakaran and his friend shot at Uma Maheswaran and another person at Pondy Bazaar in Chennai. The shoot-out that occurred was unplanned in all probability. Prabhakaran was arrested while he was trying to flee the spot; Uma Maheswaran was arrested six days later near a railway station.

The jubilant Sri Lankan government announced a one-million-rupee reward for the Tamil Nadu police. But the Tamil Nadu politicians would have none of it. They did not want Prabhakaran on their hands. A Chennai court on 6 August released both the militants on conditional bail ordering them to stay in different cities and report to their respective police stations. Prabhakaran was sent to Madurai. He stayed with a politician under the eyes of the police force. However, he had their vote of sympathy and he managed to renew old contacts and make new ones.

During these three years, Prabhakaran was able to open safe houses in Sirumalai, Pollachi, and Mettur. But he knew that his struggle had to be launched from Sri Lanka. So, in 1987 he left again for Jaffna, simply disappearing while he was going from Madurai to Chennai.

He has never come into Sri Lankan hands. Many Sri Lankan army commanders have tried to capture Prabhakaran: J.E.D. Perera, T.I. Weeratunge, G.N. Seneviratne, H. Wanasinghe, D.S. Attygalle, L.D.C.E. Waidyaratne, G.H. De Silva, R. de S. Daluwatte, C.S. Weerasooriya, and L.P. Balagalle. All of them have failed. Prabhakaran has walked away from their strategies unscathed and, even more, has been able to reply tit-for-tat to all of them. That a slew of commanders and governments have not been able to nab him testifies to Prabhakaran's and the LTTE's efficacy as a guerrilla force.

Sri Lankan President Chandrika Kumaratunga is not an exception. She was lucky to escape an LTTE assassination attempt during the general elections. She lost an eye.

Prabhakaran and the LTTE have gone beyond purely military

abilities – the adoption of stealth, the ability to surprise, to communicate fear and panic, to hide, to hold their own safe territory – and achieved much more.

In the arena of politics, Prabhakaran has challenged the status quo. The Tamil political leadership before Prabhakaran had only one tactic: win constituencies during the elections and use them as bargaining tools in the Sri Lankan Parliament to win footholds for Tamils.

Prabhakaran changed that. To admirers, he is often seen as having followed two Asian masters – Mao Tse-tung and Vo Nguyen Giap, the chief of the Vietnamese army – in that he spoke directly to the wielders of power by immobilising those who made their power secure: the army and the police. He was helped in this by the fact that by the 1970s the Sri Lankan security establishment had been converted into a 99 per cent Sinhala-Buddhist enterprise and it was therefore easier for the militants to train their guns on it. There was hardly any compunction about politicians too – their discriminatory policies already fuelled much of the Tamilian and the Tigers' fury. In brief, the establishment came under heavy fire. It still does.

Whenever the two warring parties have talked, they have not been able to reach an understanding. The first peace talks were held in Bhutan in July 1985. Five years later, the Premadasa government began negotiations with the LTTE. Fourteen months of talking peace ended when the LTTE resumed the separatist war. A third round of talks began in October of 1994. But on 19 April 1995 the LTTE said goodbye to all that when it bombed two Sri Lankan navy boats.

Then on 6 September 1998, the Tigers took the initiative and made a peace-talk offer on the condition that the talks would be held under third-party mediation. But the government rejected the offer.

The latest peace-talk move involves the Norwegians. They have been to Jaffna and had detailed discussions about devolution of power to the Tamils. The mediation effort hit a roadblock in April 2001 but the new government headed by Prime Minister Ranil Wickremesinghe asked Norway to continue its efforts. The Prime Minister began peace talks with the LTTE and lifted economic sanctions on the movement of goods to LTTE areas, continuing with the plan drawn by the previous government. In fact, the Norwegian mediation seems to have broken new ground between the LTTE and the government this year and has brokered a ceasefire.

But Velupillai Prabhakaran's struggle has seen peace efforts before and those who know him say his fight would end only when his cause is attained. However this struggle may be judged, and it can only be judged after time has given the island nation some reprieve, some pause for peace, its one indisputable achievement will be this: that it brought the Tamil cause to light and proved that it was worth fighting for. Another result of Prabhakaran's protracted war is already tangible: peace in Sri Lanka has no chance until the Tamils are counted and valued.

'When my conscience awakened, I found the love of Pakistan all around me. I gave up plans of joining the IAS to be part of the struggle.'

Syed Salahudin: Hizb-ul-Mujahideen

Zafar Meraj

His followers call him *Pir Sahib* (revered saint) out of respect and believe he has supernatural powers. Strongly contradicting their veneration, the Indian authorities mark him out amongst their Most Wanted. Mohammad Yusuf Shah alias Syed Salahudin, the supreme commander of the Hizb-ul-Mujahideen, the Kashmiri guerrilla outfit, himself attests only to his ordinariness.

'I am a common man,' he says as regards his 'powers' that, followers believe, have seen him elude capture for the last five years. 'God be witness, I have no merit on the basis of which I could claim to have been chosen for any special duty. When I look back on my life, I do not see any exploit which I can be proud of.'

Indeed Syed Salahudin's early life does not go out of the way to upset the common-man image. He was born in the winter of 1946 at Soya Bug, a village in the Kashmir Valley, in the home of Syed Ghulam Rasool Shah Farooqi. However, Soya Bug was not Salahudin's ancestral village. His father Ghulam Rasool belonged to village Takya Shah Farooq in Budgam district. Salahudin was the seventh child of his parents. His mother was not happy at his birth: she was already fed up with the six who had come before him.

During Salahudin's childhood, Syed Ghulam Din Shah, who was a religious scholar in Soya Bug took Salahudin under his guardianship. Syed Ghulam Din Shah was carrying on the religious legacy of his father Syed Ahmad Shah, who was also a religious scholar. Din Shah had also reared Salahudin's father, imparted religious and spiritual knowledge to him and transferred his spiritual legacy to him.

But the person from whom Syed Salahudin was given a hint of his final destination was neither a spiritual master in the defined sense of the term nor a member of any particular spiritual order. His name was Maulana Saeed-ud-Din, and he was of the Jamaat-e-Islami (JeI), the political and ideological partner of the Hizb-ul-Mujahideen.

However, Syed Salahudin's formal education, began with his admission to the Soya Bug middle school. Initially, he was inclined towards medical science and took up related subjects but soon after finishing school thought of taking the Indian Administrative Services Examination. After graduating from Sri Partap College in 1968, he enrolled in the Kashmir University for a Master of Arts degree in political science.

It was at Sri Partap College that Salahudin was introduced to the JeI, though the organisation was not unknown to him. He knew of many important persons who were with the JeI. Maulana Ghulam Nabi Nisar, the head-teacher at the high school, was a JeI member. Similarly, there was Ghulam Nabi Mir, a *rukn* (basic member) of JeI (who is in jail these days) and Dr Mohammad Sultan. These members had exemplary personalities and a singular and convincing style of preaching. But Salahudin was still unaware of the programme of the JeI.

One day, on returning from college he dropped in at the JeI office on Maisuma road in Srinagar where he met Maulana Saeed-ud-Din. The encounter is best described in his own words: 'As soon as I got sight of Maulana Saeed-ud-Din's face, my heart cried out that this is the face of a *Momin* (a true, practising Muslim) and this is a favoured person of Allah. His face gleamed with such a brightness of faith that I was enamoured by him no sooner than I had seen him.'

These were the last days of the sixties. After facts and arguments had won over Salahudin, he devoted himself to serving the JeI. He decided to shoulder the task of spreading its ideas, initially in college and then in the university.

Salahudin had himself felt a need for propagating Islamic literature to fight secular ideas. This led him to a deeper study of Islam. He took advantage of his command of the English language and his ability to address gatherings. Gradually, his arguments began to influence students and teachers. His efforts led many youths to join the Jamaat. He managed to hold prayers in the university premises. He started a movement to persuade women Muslim students to veil themselves. There were 20 women students in the department of political science. Barring a few, all accepted the idea. Syed Salahudin also set up a small library in the university to provide Islamic literature.

Salahudin's family had always favoured the concept of Kashmir's liberation and slowly, he began to hate India. One incident firmed his attitude. He relates it himself: 'Close to the Hokarsar lake, there is a vast field on a hillock. The children from the village used this field as their playground. When I bought a motorcycle, I went there to practise riding. At that time, this land was lying unused. Some people used to plough part of it to grow black cumin and the Indian Army had occupied the rest of it to build barracks. When I reached there, a soldier came out of a barrack and contemptuously ordered me not to ride the motorcycle there. I was surprised but he did not give me any reason although the place was not connected to the barracks in any respect. My right on it could not be challenged. On that day, for the first time I realised intensely that we were the subjugated people. India had enslaved us. I returned, very disappointed . . .'

Syed Salahudin says, 'When my conscience began to awaken, I found the love for Pakistan all around me. Pakistan's love was in the soil of Kashmir and except for those whose faces carried the seal of treason on them, every Kashmiri was ready to die for Pakistan. At school, when my concept of freedom was still not very clear, the love of Pakistan flowed in my veins like blood. I remember very well: on 14 August 1965, we celebrated the Independence Day of Pakistan and chanted slogans like "Pakistan zindabaad." The next day, that is, India's Independence day on August 15 we staged a protest demonstration against India in which we waved black flags.'

When Salahudin was at college, he took out processions in support of Pakistan, held pro-Pakistan seminars in the university and suffered at the hands of the police. He delivered speeches criticising the Indian system and highlighting the merits of the Islamic way of life. Though he knew his job very well by that time, he had not determined where to go. He needed a *khizr*. (A *khizr* is a prophet who has been allowed by the Almighty to live on earth until the Day of Judgment; his duty is to guide those who go astray.)

Salahudin was gifted with a leader's qualities and a preacher's characteristics. To his friends and teachers he had proved his varied personality. He was intelligent; everyone at home liked him and he was also popular among the village's younger generation. However, he was no different from thousands of young men and women who dream of senior official posts, and immediately after the completion of their education begin to prepare for it.

Syed Salahudin was still determined to appear in the Indian Administrative Services Examination. Though he hated the Indian system, he had not thought of a way out. While he was preparing for the IAS exam, something happened that would change his life and revolutionise the role of the JeI. The Jamaat leaders sought his help when a teacher at the JeI school in Srinagar's Nawab Bazaar, suddenly left to take up a government job, leaving nearly 150 students in the lurch. The Jamaat administration could not find a suitable person and Salahudin's name was suggested. The leader of the Srinagar JeI, Nazeer Ahmad, and another Jamaat functionary, Ashiq Kashmiri, who was a poet and author, went to Soya Bug to meet Salahudin. Salahudin agreed only in part to their request: he would take just those classes that were at their last stages. Since he wanted to join the Indian civil service after that, he asked the administration to relieve him after six months.

Salahudin says he accepted the responsibility because he 'feared the loss that the students would face. Every now and again that teacher who had left a religious school in pursuit of some fringe benefits and had jeopardised the future of so many students aroused my anger.' So, Salahudin started to go to school and teach.

His monthly salary was Rs 120. Far more important was the chance he had to observe and listen to the leaders of the Jamaat, including Maulana Saeed-ud-Din. Salahudin completed six months in the school with the students performing well in their exams and when he went to take his leave of the Maulana, he was asked about his future plans. When told of them, he asked: 'Is that all?'

'We have no objection to that,' the Maulana continued. 'But you should think it over before you leave, and then decide whether you would like to serve an evil system or the God and his prophet?' It was a decisive moment in Salahudin's life. He gave the Maulana the answer he wanted: 'Sir, from today onwards, I will serve my Allah only.'

Syed Salahudin's time to serve came soon. Elections for the Kashmir assembly were to be held in 1972. The Jamaat had put up a few candidates but it had no candidate in Budgam, the native place of Salahudin. The Jamaat had a poor record of fieldwork in this district too and its representation was minimal in terms of number of members and their political and religious activities. Mirza Arif Baig a retired director of Radio Kashmir and close relative of Mirza Afzal Baig, the President of the Plebiscite Front was contesting as an independent. Realising that it was impossible to run the election campaign without the support of the Jamaat, he contacted them and promised to work as their member in the Assembly and follow its manifesto in toto if they supported him.

The Jamaat decided to cooperate. Since most Jamaat members in that constituency were government employees they were unable to extend any help in the election campaign. Syed Salahudin was still not in the administrative body of the Jamaat but was chosen to go to the people for their votes.

With a vehicle and a hand-held loudspeaker, Syed Salahudin started his political career formally. Knocking at every door was an experience that taught him how to sway people. There were innumerable villages and settlements in the Budgam constituency. With his oratorical charm, Salahudin pointed out the contradictions in the letter and spirit of the Congress and the National Conference. He spoke of the JeI as a religious and pro-freedom party.

He ran a successful election campaign for about a month but the results were not in favour of Mirza Arif Baig. Still Baig polled some three or four thousand votes. In a constituency where the Jamaat members were hardly around forty, this was a haul. However, the success of the Jamaat lay in that its message spread to places where its name had not been heard of. Salahudin had proved his mettle as a Jamaat member. Soon, he was given more responsibilities. He not only become a *rukn* of the Jamaat, but was also made the deputy chief of sub-district Budgam. What others achieved in years, Salahudin achieved in days.

After having served at the Budgam sub-district, he was promoted to the post of Secretary General (*qayyam*) Budgam district. Srinagar and Budgam were in the same district at that time. When Srinagar and Budgam were split into two separate districts, Salahudin was made the chief of district Srinagar and Ismail Butt (later killed) became the chief of Budgam district.

Following the imposition of the Emergency by Prime Minister Indira Gandhi in 1975, the Jamaat, like most other organisations, was banned but it reorganised itself under a new name – the Islami Tahreek-e-Talaba or Islamic Students Movement. Syed Salahudin was selected as its *Nazim-e-ala*, the Chief Executive. It was the strongest student organisation, enrolling thousands of members from schools, colleges and universities. It gave its members a clear agenda on freedom and Islam and initiated a decisive phase for the youth.

Salahudin became a renowned personality in public circles. Between 1972 and 1989, besides serving the Jamaat in different capacities, he continued to preach. Preaching was his constant, a mission he fulfilled while travelling, at home or outside it, at public places and in jail. He was behind bars in 1985, 1987 and 1989, on charges of preaching sedition and what the authorities termed 'anti-national activities'.

In 1987, Syed Salahudin decided to contest an election on the ticket of the Muslim Mutahidda Mahaaz or Muslim United Front (MUF), a joint front put up by nearly a dozen separatist political and other groups including JeI, to fight the National Conference-Congress alliance. Salahudin's constituency was Srinagar's prestigious Amirakadal. People extended their full support to him. Syed Salahudin reportedly got 95 per cent of the votes, but the Government of India declared Ghulam Mohiuddin Shah of the National Conference the winner, amidst allegations of rigging and bogus polling. Salahudin and his excited supporters were arrested. The counting of votes was postponed for a couple of days. And when all the MUF leaders were in jail, Mohiuddin Shah and others like him were declared successful. Mohiuddin Shah reportedly had not dared enter his own constituency even once. The Jamaat suspected the results were hijacked.

After nine months, following a High Court verdict that proclaimed their detention illegal, the government freed Salahudin and other leaders. After he was released, Salahudin resumed his office as the chief of Srinagar district. Beginning a tradition, he also started to address congregations in the Jamia Mosque in the city's central market, propagating jihad. This was unbearable for official authorities. So in early 1989 he was again arrested and sent to jail. Salahudin spent another nine months in Srinagar Central Jail. But now he was not helpless. Outside the jail, his companions, disciples and devotees had started a jihad for freedom. He was still in jail when the Hizb-ul-Mujahideen was established.

While Salahudin was in Srinagar jail, prisoners of the Big Jail, as the separatists classified the Kashmir Valley, had started an armed freedom movement. Trained and untrained mujahideen, carrying the flags of numerous large and small jihadi organisations, had joined the movement. Simultaneously, the Jammu and Kashmir Liberation Force (JKLF) also became active. Those present in the frontline in JKLF were those who had run Syed Salahudin's election campaign.

Salahudin learnt about the establishment of the Hizb-ul-Mujahideen, the organisation whose leadership was to be conferred upon him, through a newspaper in jail. Other militant groups like Al-Badr and Allah Tigers were already active and Syed Salahudin was not only aware of their jihadi activities but also gave them ideological guidance. In the middle of 1989, it was decided that all these groups should be merged for setting up the Hizb-ul-Mujahideen. There was much consideration as regards the name of the new organisation. At length, its name was coined from two jihadi movements – the Tahreek-ul-Mujahideen and the Hizb-e-Islami.

Around that time Syed Salahudin was released once again on a High Court verdict. He set out for home with the police on his tail. Keen to avoid capture, Salahudin went into hiding, thus inaugurating his jihadi career. He also decided to participate actively in the armed jihad.

Several jihadi organisations and groups had come into being

before the Hizb-ul-Mujahideen was set up. All the 'freedom fighters' were affiliated with one organisation or the other. Every now and then new groups appeared and disappeared. The People's League, Al-Umar Mujahideen, Allah Tigers and JKLF, to name a few, were strong militant groups. At this stage, the establishment of a new organisation was apparently an unnecessary addition. But the organisation that had the support of the JeI and whose leader was Syed Salahudin soon proved it was different. In fact, the foundation of the Hizb-ul-Mujahideen was an important event in the militant history of Kashmir.

At first, the chief patron was a seemingly strange post, unknown to military organisations. In fact, the post was a tribute to their leader by those who were in the vanguard of the armed jihad. They included commanders Maqbool Illahi, Ashraf Dar, Shams-ul-Haq, Abdullah Bangro, Nasir-ul-Islam, Ahsan Dar, Waheed Sheikh, Ijaz Dar and Imran Rahi. Ahsan Dar was appointed the chief commander of the Hizb-ul-Mujahideen.

Nasir-ul-Islam (now dead) was its ameer or chief. Syed Salahudin was not only the leader of the Hizb-ul-Mujahideen, he worked as a contact person between all pro-freedom organisations, and their members who had different dispositions and ideas. His charismatic personality soon attracted other jihadi organisations that merged with the Hizb-ul-Mujahideen.

For the Hizb-ul-Mujahideen to expand, it was essential that it have a strong connection with its base camp. Moreover, it was necessary to establish a network and constantly communicate with the supporters and sympathisers of jihad in Kashmir. As the organisation's leader, Syed Salahudin wanted to acquire military training and the know-how of modern guerrilla warfare. This was impossible while he was busy on the frontline. Therefore in the beginning of November 1990 he visited the base camp, in Pakistan Occupied Kashmir. He had set out on his journey from Srinagar during the last days of October. Ill health, snow and the Indian patrolling of the Line of Control (LoC) were great hurdles in his way.

Once there, he made concerted efforts to strengthen Kashmir's jihadi warfront and so also went to Afghanistan for guerrilla training. During his stay there, Salahudin also met Afghan leaders to learn from their experiences of guerrilla warfare. He learnt of the tactics that the Afghans had used to knock out the Russians. He realised Kashmir's mujahideen had a lot to learn.

Importantly, the Afghan mujahideen were also willing to fight with the Kashmiri militants. Afghan leaders, Gulbadin Hikmatyar and Professor Burhanuddin Rabbani, assured Salahudin in personal as well as public meetings that the Afghan nation would leave no stone unturned in fully supporting the demand for a Kashmiri nation.

Before returning to Kashmir in October 1991, Salahudin had completed his mission satisfactorily. Training in modern arms had been vital for the leader of the Hizb-ul-Mujahideen. Immediately, he could also arrange for the training of recruits in an improved manner after taking into account the advice of JeI leaders in 'Azad Kashmir' or POK (Pakistan Occupied Kashmir – the terminology depends on which side of the border you are on: thus, fighters are either militants or mujahideen, martyred or slain). In long sittings, he discussed at length what was required for active jihad in Kashmir with his supporters.

In Salahudin's absence, the militant cause had suffered. The Indian security agencies had increased their military presence. It was imperative that the jihad be intensified. The mujahideen were in high spirits, better trained and well armed. Today, in fact, the jihad in Kashmir has reached a stage where guns and Kalashnikovs have been reduced to being defence tools only, according to Salahudin. But, more than ever before, the militants needed a leadership with a far better vision of the distant future.

During this time, Ahsan Dar wanted to be relieved of his duties as the chief commander of the Hizb-ul-Mujahideen. Though there were many reasons for this, the primary cause was that Ahsan Dar did not accept the advisory system of the Hizb-ul-Mujahideen. On more than one occasion, he had articulated his desire to take decisions on his own. The Hizb-ul-Mujahideen, on the other hand, followed the Quranic edict which asks even the Holy Prophet to seek the advice of his fellows before taking a decision and then to tell the Muslims to follow his footsteps. But Dar had insisted frequently on a free hand.

At the initial stages, when the administrative body of the Hizb-ul-Mujahideen was small, such an attitude was tolerable. However, with the expansion of its network, the tendency for a single person to take a decision began to cause problems for the high command of the JeI. So Dar resigned and expressed his desire to work as an ordinary soldier. The decision was accepted.

However, matters did not settle even after his departure. The leaders of the Islamic movement then decided to put the burden of the leadership on Salahudin. The office of the supreme commander was made his responsibility.

Salahudin immediately made structural changes in the Hizb-ul-Mujahideen. Until that time, its structure was not very different from ordinary military and political organisations. Under Salahudin, however, the largest organisation of freedom fighters was restructured on the latest military lines.

On 3 November 1991, the advisory council of the Hizb-ul-Mujahideen dissolved offices such as those of the chief guardian, ameer and secretary general and entrusted the central command to the supreme commander completely. Other changes followed. Syed Salahudin was appointed the supreme commander and his confidant and ex-secretary general of the Hizb-ul-Mujahideen, Abdul Majid Dar, was made adviser general to the supreme commander. The central command was also reorganised. A comprehensive command system was devised. Different sections, such as the launching wing, education wing, intelligence wing, and revenue wing among others, were given to different commanders. An advisory board was instituted to stop individual decisions and check individual wilfulness. At the same time, the advisory system was broadened beyond the centre, to the levels of a division, battalion, company and platoon. In the new system, divisions were set up, each comprising two to three districts. Each division and district was given to the divisional and district commanders respectively.

Under the leadership of Salahudin, the Hizb-ul-Mujahideen emerged as the most powerful militant group, not only in Kashmir but also in the Jammu region. He organised Hizb cadres in areas like Doda, Poonch and Rajouri besides creating a separate unit to take on Indian forces in the Pirpanjal mountains that divide Jammu and Kashmir. Salahudin's era also saw Hizb militants undertake crucial actions. In one case, the Hizb blew up the telephone transmission towers set up atop a high mountain near Banihal. It was in late 1992 and as a result, STD facilities in the entire Kashmir Valley remained cut off for several months. The Hizb, in defence, said that their action hampered the activities of the Indian security forces as they were unable to communicate with their counterparts across the mountain.

The abortive attempt made on the life of the Kashmir Governor General (Retd) K V Krishna Rao on 26 January 1995 is the one which the Hizb is still identified with. The attack came on India's Republic Day, when Rao was addressing the ceremonial parade in Jammu. In the midst of his speech, a deafening explosion took place after a powerful device planted just under the podium exploded. Though Rao had a miraculous escape, nearly a dozen people on duty around the podium at that time were killed.

As the activities of the Hizb started gaining momentum, the Indian authorities mobilised all their resources to zero in on Salahudin. Pressure mounted on the Hizb cadre, especially Salahudin, with the result that he was virtually confined to a few selected hideouts. With no free movement possible for him, Salahudin developed ailments and his friends, both in Kashmir and across the border, advised him to visit the 'base camp'. A reluctant Salahudin agreed after much persuasion

In mid-1995 he crossed over to 'Azad Kashmir', from where he now commands his 'boys' in Kashmir. Salahudin is reported to have set up a communication network using the latest technology to keep in touch with his commanders in Jammu and Kashmir. Though authorities, at least on three occasions, claimed to have destroyed the Hizb network, its main communication centre remains active.

Due to the keen interest shown by Salahudin, Hizb cadres were armed with the latest weapons during the last eight years. Today, the Hizb is the most powerful and probably the only indigenous Kashmiri militant group though it has quite a few foreigners, including fighters from Pakistan and Afghanistan, in its cadre. The group likes to propagate the view that its local Kashmiri commanders lead their respective groups and are authorised to take decisions on their own, but intelligence reports suggest that some of them feel like second-rate militants because they often end up as guides and couriers for the foreign mercenaries. Although the strength of the Hizb has gone down to some extent in recent years, especially, after the emergence of foreign groups like Lashkar-e-Toiba, Harkat-ul-Mujahideen and Jaish-e-Mohammed, rough estimates suggest that the Hizb still has between 1000 and 1500 members who are active on the ground. Though the Hizb men mark their presence at times by attacking Indian security personnel, the fact remains that activities have shown a marked decline after Lashkar and Harkat and lately the Jaish captured the front rows.

The feeling of being reduced to second-rung militants, perhaps, led to the announcement of a ceasefire in July 2000. Salahudin's close lieutenant, Majid Dar, made the dramatic announcement in Srinagar and expressed their willingness to talk to New Delhi. Dar's announcement caught everybody by surprise including, according to insiders, Salahudin. Though Dar claimed that the supreme council in Pakistan had taken the ceasefire decision and that Salahudin had been party to it, one view is that Dar had not taken the leadership into confidence. Salahudin supported Dar but laid down conditions that were difficult for New Delhi to accept. Willing to go ahead with a dialogue, Salahudin said it would be possible only if Pakistan too was made a party to the talks. The ceasefire call was withdrawn within two weeks, some say at the behest of the Pakistani establishment.

Reports suggest that the ceasefire announcement led to serious differences between Salahudin and Majid Dar. Those close to Salahudin say that he believes that any solution of the Kashmir issue should not look as if it was being thrust on the people of Kashmir and that peace should be brought back to the Valley with 'honour and dignity'. In Dar's offer, Salahudin is said to have sensed a sell-out and that prompted his criticism.

As the commander of the Hizb-ul-Mujahideen, Salahudin faced many more problems while implementing his strategy of jihad. Internal and external pressures continuously dogged him. However, the Hizb cadres believe that Salahudin was instrumental in devising unique guerrilla tactics that saw India suffer financially. For one, Indian security forces had to spend to rehabilitate and maintain military installations, bridges and the mobile units that were destroyed.

Indian soldiers set various traps to capture Salahudin but he eluded them each time. It is reported that even they began to believe that Salahudin had *shakti* or supernatural powers. Indeed, he appears to have extricated himself out of seemingly inescapable situations. Some unseen hand shattered the plans of the enemy every time, interpret his supporters, as if the sieges were just fragile spider webs. These may all be myths but are stories that motivate the cadre.

One such incident saw him and those with him escape fire from a very close range. After Salahudin had become the commander of the Hizb-ul-Mujahideen, he visited an area called Harooni, near a dense forest and a farm named Dachigaam. Mujahideen from the surrounding area had gathered to meet him. Salahudin addressed two gatherings and met the mujahideen individually, giving important instructions to their commanders and briefing them about their targets.

After the meeting, he left, taking the same path that passes through Dachigaam accompanied by the local battalion commander and some aides. They stopped at a rest house in the thick jungle and sent an aide to the bazaar for food and travel accessories. When he did not return for a long time, everybody was worried. The local commander and two other men hired a vehicle to go to the bazaar to look for him, but nearly a quarter of an hour passed without a word coming from them. Salahudin was anxious by this time. Suddenly the party heard shots in the distance. Indian soldiers were firing constantly at them from just 30 metres away. The bullets were being fired from such a close distance that it was impossible for anyone to escape getting hurt. However, strangely no one was hit, although there was neither any shelter nor any time to take shelter. The militants decided to flee the place immediately and within a few moments they had all escaped.

Salahudin recounts this experience himself: 'Running through a hail of bullets we took refuge in the jungle. We spent the daytime hiding there and at night took to a distant shelter. The enemy could get no clue for three days and three nights. Our Lord made the enemy go back hopeless and at a loss.'

Another such event occurred in a jungle near Pulwama from where Salahudin was operating in those days. His wife had come to meet him at their second meeting in three years at a house in a village near the jungle. Before night fell, Salahudin reached his destination on horseback. His wife was already there.

Next morning, when he was preparing to return, his security staff told him that a large number of troops were coming to surround the village. He quickly disappeared and twenty minutes later, the Indian Army entered that safe house. By that time Salahudin and his aides were several miles away. The Army questioned the locals. They talked to his wife but did not know whom they were talking to. They had missed a great opportunity.

It is not only in the matter of warfare that Salahudin's bravery is fabled. His life is seen as one that has withstood great change. From a person who had spent 45 years in cities, doing *imamat* (holding the office of an imam), relishing oratory, teaching students, and leading a family life he became the leader of the Hizb-ul-Mujahideen. He began living in jungles and deserted places, cut off from the world, from worldly comforts and pleasures and from familial ties.

Salahudin has not minded the changes. He says, 'I long to go to every village and every house in the state of Jammu and Kashmir and meet my brothers, sisters, elders and children. But my mission demands that I hide in jungles and remain cut off from my fellow beings.'

Salahudin's commitment to jihad has forced him to do without many other things. For one, sleep. He goes to bed late at night and wakes up early in the morning. He prays at his hideout regularly and in a congregation leads the prayers himself. He is a skilled orator, of course, and recites the Quran with an impassioned voice. During the morning prayers, his style makes his comrades forget at least temporarily their violent world. Salahudin frequently recites the *surah* of Al-Saf (the rank) in the Morning Prayer that is especially instructive for the devotees.

Prayer is, in fact, a form of relief for Salahudin. When his heart is heavy, he finds solace and peace in prayer. He relishes such moments. All grief is overcome at such times. It appears to him as if Allah's mercy has covered the whole atmosphere.

Leading the Hizb-ul-Mujahideen has been a strange experience for Salahudin. Especially since he started as a school teacher and went on to head a militant organisation. As its military man, he devised strategy that kept the security forces on their toes for he decided that the militants would target them in relatively uninhabited territory. This forced the Army to hunt for the militants in difficult terrain – in jungles and in mountains. But since this was not always possible, the local population's support seemed to ebb when the Hizb resorted to the killings of the Hindu Pandits and when they often sought shelter in homes at gun point.

Salahudin is still the supreme commander of the Hizb but is at the mercy of the Pakistan establishment; for there is little that he can do as long as he is on their soil. Amongst the Most Wanted in the list of twenty, submitted to Pakistan by the Indian government, Salahudin is a virtual prisoner; and though he is still in communication with his cadre in the Kashmir Valley, he is not his own master. His strength, however, is that he heads a group that is seen as indigenous and not one dominated by foreign mercenaries.

Annexure I

Excerpts from Omar Sheikh's interrogation report:

1. *Name – Ahmed Umar Saeed Sheikh @ Rohit Sharma @ Aamir @ Khalid.*
2. *Father's Name – Syed Ahmed Sheikh, Originally from Lahore, DOB: 1948. Runs a wholesale readymade garments business, has a Fashion Store in London.*
3. *Qualification – Studied up to 2nd-year B.Sc in London School of Economics.*
4. *Nationality – British/Pakistani.*
5. *Description – Round face, small beard, small nose, fair complexion, black eyes and stout built.*
6. *Languages known – English, Urdu, Arabic and Punjabi.*

Brief History

The subject was born on 23 December 1973 in London. At the age of five, he was admitted to Nightingale Primary School. After two years, the subject was shifted to Forest School. While studying there, the subject took part in the London Chess Championship (in the under-nine age group). He was granted a scholarship for 6,000 pounds per year for his good grades in Forest School.

Since his childhood, the subject has been aggressive and always indulged in fights with his other English schoolmates for their sarcastic racial remarks. He never tolerated any remarks against Islam and was against racial discrimination, particularly against anyone calling him 'Paki' (the word is commonly used by the whites against the Asian migrants). The subject was suspended twice from the school, at first for one week and, then, for two days for fighting with the white classmates over some racial remarks. These developments inculcated a sense of hostility in the subject who was always ready for a fight on the slightest provocation. He remained in Forest School till the age of fourteen.

First Visit to Pakistan

After leaving school in September 1987, the subject and his family migrated to Pakistan. The subject joined Aitchison College, Lahore. He remained in Pakistan from September 1987 to December 1990 and completed Senior Cambridge and Higher Secondary/Pre-University there. In December 1990, he went back to London alone for further studies. The subject's father contacted Forest School in London for his re-admission. While studying in Forest School, he did very well and earned good grades. In the school, he received several awards for extracurricular activities. From January 1991 to June 1992, he remained in Forest School.

Second Visit to Pakistan

In June 1992, the subject again went to Pakistan to bring his family. After two months in Pakistan, the subject returned to London around September 1992.

Admission to London School of Economics

After coming back from Pakistan, the subject started preparing for admission to universities. He applied in Harvard and Stanford, both American universities, but could not get in. Finally, he managed to get admission in the first-year B.Sc course in the London School of Economics. His subjects were Economics, Statistical Theory and Application and Mathematical Calculation. While studying there, the subject went to Geneva to take part in the world level Arms Wrestling Championship in October 1992. In Geneva, the subject met an Indian by the name of Brij Baran Das. His address in India is 65, Sharat Bose Road, Calcutta. The subject could not disclose any important information about him. The subject had, however, given the name of Das in the reference column of his visa application to the Indian High Commission, London. The subject stayed in Geneva for a week and returned to London in October 1992. The subject once again took part in the London Arms Wrestling Championship and scored fifth position in the middle-class category.

Joining Islamic Society

During his first year in the London School of Economics, in October 1992, the subject joined the Islamic Society immediately after returning from Geneva. Shaukat, originally a Pakistani, was the president of the organisation. His wife's name is Amreen, who is also Pakistani. The general secretary of the Society was some Malaysian girl. The aim of the organisation is to work for Islam. It had about 100 members – all Muslim students of the London School of Economics. While in school, the subject used to attend/listen to lectures on Islam organised by the Society. Hussain Nawaz Sharif, son of former PM of Pakistan, Nawaz Sharif, was also a friend of the subject and was studying in the same school. Hussain Nawaz Sharif contested the election for the post of general secretary of Islamic Society in LSE but was defeated by the Malaysian girl. The Muslim students used to contribute three pounds per annum to the Islamic Society and about 800 to 900 pounds per annum were received from the school authorities. The Islamic societies function in all colleges/universities in UK where Muslims students are enrolled.

Observance of Bosnia Week

In November 1992, a Bosnia week was organised by Islamic Society with a view to raise funds for Bosnia. Various documentary films on atrocities on Bosnian Muslims were shown. Many Muslim refugees from Bosnia were invited to reveal the atrocities committed on them by the Serbs who urged the audience to help them in their just cause. The subject also saw a film named *Destruction of a Nation*. It was a 45-minute documentary that depicted the castration of Muslim prisoners in Serb detention camps. After watching Muslim children and their horrified screams and atrocities on pregnant women, the subject was emotionally disturbed. During this time, every Muslim student in the LSE, including the son of former Pakistan Prime Minister Hussain Nawaz Sharif, decided to do something for the Bosnian cause. After the week was over, the subject told his father that he wanted to do something for the cause. By that time, the subject had lost his peace of mind and the issue was constantly bothering him. The parents of the subject advised him not to get involved in such acts.

The subject was of the view that lecturing and collecting funds was not enough as the Muslims in Bosnia continued to suffer. To achieve something tangible, the subject continued to contact people and make enquiries for going to Bosnia. In the process, he came to know that about 20 Muslim youth from England in the age group of 20-45 years had gone to Bosnia. He further disclosed that a majority of the militants fighting in Bosnia were Arabs, who had earlier fought in Afghanistan.

Involvement with Muslim Aid and Islamic Relief

For the purpose of doing something for the victims of Bosnia, the subject joined Muslim Aid and Islamic Relief agencies in UK. These two agencies were involved in providing aid and also raising funds in London for Bosnian Muslims. Cat Stevens, a pop singer who had converted to Islam and acquired the name Yusuf, was the president of Islamic Relief.

Bosnia Conference

While working with the above two organisations, the subject decided to organise a conference in London as a part of his efforts to contribute to the Bosnian cause. He approached all London universities and requested them to help organise functions for Bosnia. The subject, with the active assistance of other representatives, was successful in bringing all colleges together for this conference. Diplomats and speakers from all Islamic countries were invited to the conference. Apart from this, some refugees from Bosnia were also requested to participate and share their experiences in the conference.

In January/February 1993, the Bosnia conference was organised. The subject was one of the representatives and remained instrumental in organising the conference. As an active representative, the subject wrote letters and issued statements to the press. Diplomats from not more than eight countries took part in the conference. Iranian and Pakistani diplomats also participated. The conference was a big success as about one thousand people participated. A number of resolutions were passed. Umar Bakri Muhammad, chief, Party of Liberation, emphasised that Bosnia and Kashmir were serious matters of concern for the Islamic countries who should whole-heartedly and earnestly help the Bosnian people in their struggle. In the conference, religious slogans were frequently raised to arouse the feelings of the participants.

Third Visit to Pakistan

After the conference was over, the subject felt that nothing concrete had emerged and no follow-up action had been contemplated. Soon after the conference, the subject went to Pakistan with his father carrying some videos on Bosnia. It was his father's business trip. The subject showed the cassettes on Bosnia in Aitchison College.

During this period, the subject attended a rally organised by the Jamiat-ul-Ulema, Pakistan (Fazlur Rehman group) near the Jung Newspaper Office at Lahore. During the question round, the subject asked Fazlur Rehman for his stand on Bosnia and was not satisfied with the replies.

Association with Convoy of Mercy

Not satisfied with his efforts for the Bosnia cause, the subject joined another relief group called the Convoy of Mercy around March 1993. Being run by Asad Khan, a Pakistani national, the organisation was involved in sending relief supplies to Bosnia through trucks. Asad Khan was also involved in clandestinely sending mujahideen to Bosnia through the convoy.

Through Asad Khan, the subject met another Pakistani national named Abdul Rauf in Bosnia. Rauf ran a militant camp and had already fought in Afghanistan and Kashmir. In Bosnia, Rauf told him that he could not fight in Bosnia since he was not trained and so before he left Bosnia, Rauf gave the subject a sealed envelope addressed to Maulana Syed-ul-Rehman. Rauf also told him to contact Maulana Ismail in London.

Influenced by Rauf's views, the subject decided to undergo

arms training in Afghanistan. The parents of the subject were shocked to see him on his return. He had become more religious and had started keeping a beard. He lost interest in studies and started talking to his parents about his proposed visit to Afghanistan for arms training. The subject claimed that his parents were not in favour of arms training in Afghanistan but he was determined to undergo the same.

In July 1993, the subject along with his father met Maulana Ismail. Both of them had discussions on arms training in Afghanistan and the subject was thoroughly briefed by Maulana Ismail. After the meeting, the subject decided to go for training to Afghanistan.

Comments: Maulana Masood Azhar in his interrogation had also admitted to having met Maulana Ismail in London. Maulana Ismail of HUA, London, had procured a Portuguese passport for Azhar through his contacts.

Fourth Visit to Pakistan

In July 1993, the subject left England for Pakistan by Gulf Air carrying 800 pounds. The subject landed at Karachi Airport and from there, he boarded another flight for Lahore. After reaching Lahore, the subject, as instructed by Rauf, went to meet Maulana Syed-ul-Rehman and handed over the letter. Rehman asked the subject to go to HUA office at Islamabad and meet Maulana Abdullah, which he did.

Next day, arrangements were made to send the subject to Miranshah office of the Harkat-ul-Ansar, located near Al Kuwaiti Hospital. From the Islamabad office, one person named Aurangzeb was asked to accompany the subject. Both of them went to Miranshah by road. Miranshah is a place where arms and ammunitions are openly sold and is a major drug smuggling point. Next day, the subject was sent to the training camp in Khost, Afghanistan.

The subject underwent training from August 1993 to December 1993. Initially, the subject joined a small weapons course but it did not appeal to him. After two weeks of training, the subject fell ill and came back to Lahore for treatment. During the treatment, the subject was advised by his relatives not to get involved in training as it would not serve any purpose. But after 10 days of treatment, the subject went back to the training camp in Afghanistan. He completed a basic weapons course in which he learnt how to handle the AK-47s, LMGs and rocket launchers. The subject was also trained to lay ambushes, and taught the art of secret meetings and surveillance and night movement. There were two types of courses at the training camp – a 14-day small weapons course and a 4-month advanced course, also called Zindula. The Zindula course was for those militants who were prepared to sacrifice their lives for the cause of Islam. On completion of his training, the subject was asked to join as instructor at the training camp and showed his willingness to join but only after meeting his parents. His other worry was that his British passport was expiring and he wanted to proceed to UK to get a new passport.

During the training, Maulana Abdullah and Maulana Masood Azhar, secretary general of the Harkat-ul-Ansar, paid a visit and held discussions with the militants including the subject. The subject had been highly influenced by listening to the recorded speeches of Maulana Azhar at the training camp.

Meeting with Maulana Masood Azhar

After completing his training in December 1993, the subject was again approached by Maulana Masood Azhar and Maulana Abdullah. Azhar told him that many people were already fighting in Bosnia and mentioned that a plan had to be executed in India shortly and solicited his services for the plan. Azhar disclosed to the subject that some VIPs were to be kept under surveillance and asked him to go back to London and get an Indian visa.

While in London, the subject received a call from Maulana Abdullah from the Islamabad HUA office, saying that Azhar had been arrested in India. He requested the subject to approach Amnesty International for pressuring India to release Azhar. Abdullah also mentioned in a telephonic call that he had also been trying, through the conference of scholars from Karachi, to pressure the Government of India for Azhar's release.

During early March 94, the subject came to know that Indian Prime Minister P.V. Narasimha Rao was visiting the UK. He started making enquiries about the details of the PM's movements. He also tried to ascertain the latter's schedule of programmes/meetings in London. His father, however, cautioned him not to take the risk of doing anything funny during the visit of the Prime Minister of India as it would jeopardise his future.

Comments: The PM visited UK on 13-16 March, 1994. The subject remained silent on the exact plans. However, he claims to have thought of a demonstration etc. to create embarrassment for both the Indian and the UK Government.

Meanwhile, he procured a European Community passport and took visas for India in March, 1994 and for Pakistan in April, 1994.

Fifth Visit to Pakistan

In May 1994, the subject again went to Pakistan and underwent a two-week refresher course at the Khalid bin Walid camp. After this course, the subject was detailed as an instructor at the same camp.

Finalisation of Kidnapping Plan

While the subject was serving as instructor at the Khalid bin Walid camp, Maulana Abdullah approached him and disclosed that a plan had been chalked out to secure the release of Sajjad Afghani and Masood Azhar. In July 1994, the subject was called to HUA office in Islamabad and the plan was discussed.

Entry into India

The subject came to Delhi on a PIA flight and checked into Holiday Inn. As planned, the subject went to Agra by a tourist bus so that he could make friends with some foreign nationals. En route the subject made acquaintance with a foreigner who later turned out to be an Israeli. His contacts in India told him that only nationals of the USA, UK and France were to be kidnapped as these countries were members of the Security

Council. The subject was asked to hunt for foreign nationals like engineers, teachers and embassy staff. He then visited the American Center, the British High Commission and its library. He then went to the main bus station in Delhi and befriended a foreign national who was making enquiries for going to Dehradun in Uttarakhand.

The subject and the foreign national boarded the bus from ISBT for Dehradun. The foreign national turned out to be an American, Richard, who was going to Dehradun to join as a teacher in Doon School. They reached Dehradun and stayed in Relax Hotel. The subject's story was that he was doing a thesis on politics and was interviewing people on links between education and politics. Next day, the subject went to Doon School and met Richard. The subject gave his name as Arindam Kumar from England (the name was also mentioned in the school register of meetings). The subject also met the principal of Doon School with Richard and requested that he be allowed to interview the students. The principal refused and the subject left, promising to meet Richard again. His contacts told him about a safe house in Saharanpur. After seeing the Saharanpur house, the subject visited Dehradun and met Richard again at Doon School. Richard was busy organising some school function and asked the subject to meet him later, so he returned to Saharanpur and came to Delhi. He kept on visiting cafes around hotels in the Pahargunj area and tried to strike up a friendship with foreign nationals. He managed in chatting up four foreigners. Two Britishers agreed to see a bit of rural India with him.

Subsequently, the subject went to Woodstock School in Mussoorie. With a view to trap an American national, the subject applied for a part time job as a teacher. He was interviewed but was not taken.

. . . The subject informed his contacts in Delhi that two Britishers were willing to go with him so they set off in a car and reached Saharanpur where two others, Salauddin and Siddique, were waiting for them with pistols and rifles. The Britishers were informed that they had been taken hostage and were chained. They were told that the purpose of their kidnapping was to carry out a specific task in India. The subject took the details of their passports and returned to Delhi where he was asked to now quickly look for an American. He was also told by his Delhi contacts that another house had been arranged in Ghaziabad for more kidnapped foreigners.

On a visit to Pahargunj, the subject met Bela Nuss, an American national. Nuss was alone and needed company. The subject exploited this and developed a friendship. The subject told Nuss that he was staying in Galaxy Hotel in Pahargunj and could meet him there. Nuss visited Galaxy Hotel in his absence and left a message for the subject to contact him in the same café in Pahargunj where they used to meet. The subject then told Bela Nuss that he had been invited the next day by one of the Indian families to dinner and he could came along. Bela Nuss, quite delighted over the offer, agreed.

The subject was told that Salaudin and Siddique had also come back from Saharanpur and was asked to select one of them as his partner in the kidnapping. The subject came to Pahargunj to take Bela Nuss with him. Bela Nuss was waiting for him with a cake for the Indian family. Next, one of the subject's companions took out a pistol and told Nuss that he had been kidnapped and should not create any scene otherwise he would be in trouble. The subject told the American national that he would be kept for some days in their custody without harm and in the meantime negotiations with the US government would be made for his release in exchange for some of their own men. A veil – *burka* – was put over Nuss, and he too was chained. The subject tried to find out the addresses of BBC, the Voice of America, the Prime Minister's Office and the American and UK embassies.

A letter was drafted for the Prime Minister of India, demanding the release of Maulana Masood Azhar and Sajjad Afghani. To substantiate the fact that they had hostages, they decided to buy a camera and take some photographs which they did. Copies were sent to the PM but they learnt from Islamabad that no exchange had taken place and so decided to send additional letters to the embassies . . . on the way back, he caught the attention of two policemen and in a shoot out, the subject was arrested while his local contacts escaped.

Annexure II

Excerpts from Masood Azhar's interrogation report:

The subject is a Pakistani national and Afghan-trained militant of the Harkat-ul-Ansar. He was holding the charge of general secretary of the organisation and was collecting funds for it. The subject was put under sustained interrogation and he stated as under:

I was born at Bahawalpur on 10 July 1968. My father was working as a headmaster in the government school at Bahawalpur. I have five brothers and six sisters. My father had a Deobandi influence and was extreme in his views. One of my father's friends, Mufti Syed, was working as a teacher in Jamia Islamia. He prevailed upon my father to admit me in the Jamia Islamia and I joined it. I passed the *almia* examination in 1989 and was immediately employed as a teacher in the Islamia where I served as a leader till April 1992.

Many students at the Jamia Islamia were under the influence of the Harkat-ul-Mujahideen (HUM). HUM was able to recruit youth for participation in the Afghan jihad. I was a sympathiser to the cause and in June/July I met HUM Amir Maulana Fazlur Rehman Khalil at Karachi. He invited me to join the party and to get trained at Yavar in Afghanistan. I went to Yavar and received training in handling Kalashnikovs and the Zoki machine-gun (a Russian machine-gun). I met Sajjad Afghani there.

I could not complete the obligatory training of 40 days and the remaining training period was waived. The Amir, Fazlur Rehman, asked me to bring out a monthly magazine for HUM.

Publishing the monthly magazine required permission from the government of Pakistan. I approached my friend Maulana Jameel, a correspondent of the Urdu daily, *Jang*, who sought permission from Pakistan on my behalf to publish *Sada-i-Mujahid*. In 1989, I started bringing out the magazine. The price was fixed at Rs five and a thousand copies were printed in a month. Most of them were distributed free during Friday prayers. The object of the magazine was to inform the people of Pakistan about the activities of HUM and the jihad taking place in Afghanistan against the Russian forces. Islamic religious teachings were also published in the magazine.

Till 1999, HUM had opened its offices at almost all the prominent cities of Pakistan, that is, Karachi, Hyderabad, Sind, Lahore, and Islamabad. HUM had recruited the youth according to three principles:

1. A recruit would undergo 40 days of arms' training at Camp Yavar in Afghanistan.
2. A recruit must not be affiliated with any social or political organisation.
3. The recruits must be bearded. Shias were not recruited; only Deobandis could join the HUM.

About Rs 800,000 were being spent on the activities of HUM; the amount being received from the public.

Earlier in 1986, I had obtained a Pakistani passport on my original name and address and used it to visit Saudi Arabia (Makka) for Umara purposes. On the directions of the chief of the Harkat-ul-Mujahideen (Khalil), I visited foreign countries for spreading HUM activities and asked for and obtained donations for the organisation there. My first such visit was in 1991 when, accompanied by Maulana Fazlur Rehman Khalil, I visited Lusaka and Chipata in Zambia. A fruit businessman in that country, Ibrahim Lambert, had invited us. I stayed in Zambia for about one month and during this period collected about Rs 2 million in Pakistani currency for the organisation in the name of religious education. In June 1992, I again visited Zambia for 20 days and collected Rs 2.2 million.

Earlier, in 1990, I and Maulvi Farooq Kashmiri visited Abu Dhabi. We succeeded in collecting donations worth Rs 10.5 million. After that we both visited Dubai and collected about Rs 200000-300000 in Pakistani currency. From Dubai, we went to Sharjah. The people of Sharjah were not interested in aiding the Kashmiri militants because they thought their relations with India were quite good. But we did get a small donation. In 1992, I again visited Sharjah and collected Rs 200000-300000.

In October 1992, I visited the UK. Mufti Ismail facilitated this visit. I stayed in UK for about one month with Mufti Ismail and visited mosques in Birmingham, Nottingham, Sheffield, and Leicester where I stayed and sought financial help. I collected Rs 1.5 million.

In 1993, international pressure was mounted on Pakistan over militancy and the Pakistani Government asked militants to leave the country. But most militants refused. Some UAE governments refused to take back the militants. A majority of them went to Sudan and then entered Somalia to join the ranks of the Ittehad-e-Islami.

The same year, in January 1993, on the instructions of Maulana Farooq Kashmiri, I visited Bangladesh. He had informed me that he wanted to send Sajjad Afghani to Kashmir through Bangladesh. Before leaving for Dhaka, I delivered speeches and made people aware about the liberation of Kashmir from Indian occupation through jihad. Sajjad Afghani also accompanied us for this trip. In this tour, Afghani was told to take up command of Kashmir operations. Along with Sajjad Afghani, we travelled by an Emirates flight to Dhaka. Afghani was sent to India.

After the formation of Harkat-ul-Ansar by the merger of HUJ and HUM, I was sent to the Valley to ascertain the ground realities and to boost the morale of the militants.

Later, I went to Dhaka and spent two days there. I reached Indira Gandhi International Airport on 29 January 1994. In February, I bought 12 compasses from Nizamuddin for the militants in Kashmir so that they could make out the directions of Makka.

On February 9, we boarded the flight for Srinagar. Ashraf Dar escorted me to Madrasa Qasmian at Lal Bazar in Srinagar and arranged a room for me. He told me that Afghani would contact me in the madrasa itself. I was taken by car to meet the militants at their hideouts. On our way back to Srinagar, the car developed some defect and we were intercepted by an Army patrol. After my arrest, Sajjad and I were taken by the

Army to a nearby camp, then to Srinagar and finally to this camp. Along with other Pak mercenaries, I was called for interrogation, but militants already lodged in this jail kept me away due to fear of torture by the IOs.

In the second week of November 1994, a plan was chalked out for digging out a tunnel. I have not taken part in digging out the tunnel but was fully aware of the fact. Other Pakistani mercenaries lodged in this jail were not aware about the episode. On November 27, jail authorities detected the tunnel. This is my statement, which is correct to the best of my knowledge.